**Gert Hirner / Jakob Murböck**

# Walks in
# Eastern Crete

**Translated by Gill Round**

50 selected day walks on the coasts and in the mountains
of Eastern Crete

With 68 colour photos,
50 small walking maps to a scale of 1: 60,000 / 1: 85,000
and an overview map to a scale of 1: 650,000

ROTHER · MUNICH

Cover photo:
Chapel on the way up from Kavoúsi to Thrípti.

Frontispiece (page 2):
Idyllic scene in front of Dikti mountain in spring.

All photos by the authors.

Cartography:
Small walking maps to a scale of 1: 60,000 / 1: 85,000
© Bergverlag Rother GmbH, Munich
(drawn by Ingenieurbüro für Kartographie Heidi Schmalfuß, Munich)
overview maps to a scale of 1: 650,000 and 1: 2,000,000
© Freytag & Berndt, Vienna

Translation:
Gill Round

1st edition 2004

© Bergverlag Rother GmbH, Munich
ISBN 3-7633-4822-0

Distributed in Great Britain by Cordee, 3a De Montfort Street, Leicester
Great Britain LE1 7HD, www.cordee.co.uk

## ROTHER WALKING GUIDES

Azores · Corsica · Côte d'Azur · Crete East, · Crete West · Cyprus · Gomera · Gran Canaria · Iceland · La Palma · Madeira · Mallorca · Mont Blanc · Norway South · Provence · Pyrenees 1 · Pyrenees 2 ·Sardinia · Sicily · High Tatra · Tenerife · Tuscany North · Valais East · Valais West · Around the Zugspitze

**Dear mountain lovers! We would be happy to hear your opinion
and suggestions for amendment to this Rother walking guide.**

### BERGVERLAG ROTHER · Munich
**D-85521 Ottobrunn • Haidgraben 3 • Tel. (089) 608669-0, Fax -69
Internet** www.rother.de · **E-mail** bergverlag@rother.de

# Foreword

Crete, the fifth largest Mediterranean island, is where the story of our western culture began. The kingdom of the Minoans, Roman, Byzantine and Venetian epochs, Turkish occupation – the cultures of the eastern Mediterranean region and of the bordering countries have intermingled here for over 5000 years and left traces behind of which the visitor to Crete is constantly aware. The abundance of cultural assets, the appealing and varied landscape, and the mild, stable climate lure holidaymakers increasingly to the Mediterranean island year after year.

The special features of the landscape, which is still unspoiled in places, the unbelievable wealth of plants, especially in the many gorges and valleys, the tranquility of the remote mountain regions and quiet plateaus, as well as the delightful coastal areas with some wonderful beaches and bays – we shouldn't allow all this to be subjected to mass tourism.

It is high time another form of travel was established that left behind fewer ugly traces and that was more socially acceptable to the inhabitants of Crete. Hiking really is the best way of getting to know the country and its people and showing some respect for the Cretans – without losing excitement, experience and relaxation in any way.

For this reason, it is a good idea to restrict yourself to one part of the island for a hiking holiday. In combination with the Rother walking guide to Crete West, this guide offers a complementary description of the finest walks in the eastern part of the island.

The walks are selected to appeal to individual interests. Stretches along the sunny coastlines, past villages and to remote monasteries are described, as well as hikes in the mountains, some of which have an alpine feel, and into narrow gorges and valleys. Special consideration is also given to walks to numerous ancient sites of which there are many more to be found in eastern Crete. The walks described in this guide are spread out over the most beautiful areas of eastern Crete and many of them are suitable for families with children.

Many of the routes were brought up to date last year, but the countryside and paths are often subject to change due to building work, new fencing and the layout of fields. The authors would therefore like to ask all friends of Crete to inform the publishers of any relevant corrections that need to be made. We wish all users of this guide many enjoyable days of adventure amidst the natural beauty of Crete.

Munich, 2003                                          Gert Hirner und Jakob Murböck

# Contents

# Tourist tips

## Use of the guide
Each walk described in the guide begins with a short fact file section containing the most important information including height variations, bus connections, or suggestions for accommodation and sometimes interesting places to visit in the area. All of the small walking maps are based on the Harms-ic maps, to a scale of 1: 100,000, with any necessary details added. In the index at the back of the book you will find all the relevant mountains, towns and villages, and the objectives of every stage of the walk. The back cover has an overview map showing the location of each of the walks.

## Grade
A quarter of the walks run along tarmac and gravel roads and a quarter over rough ground – the other half along footpaths and narrower paths. Places, where there might be some difficulty in route finding, are mentioned in the text. However, in most cases the terrain is open and the few dangerous spots, where you come near to a precipice, for example, are given special mention. But the hiker should not underestimate the particular conditions of the path like sharp-edged rock formations and scree, very prickly vegetation and lengthy stretches across sand and pebbly beaches on the coast since they make more demands on the fitness of the walker and the sturdiness of your footwear. After lengthy periods of rainfall, many of the walks are totally or partially impassable and this is mentioned in the walk description. Little used paths can be almost totally overgrown in the spring which makes route-finding more difficult and in some cases stops you from going any further. In order to assess the individual grades of the walks more accurately, the numbers of the walks have been colour-coded. The colours are explained as follows:

## BLUE
These routes are mostly well-marked and only moderately steep, and can be walked safely even in bad weather. They do not usually present any problems with route finding. They can also be undertaken by children and older people without any great danger.

## RED
These paths and mountain tracks are, as a rule, well-marked and clearly visible, but frequently narrow and they can be fairly exposed over short sections. They should only be undertaken if you are a sure-footed and fit walker.

## BLACK
These mountain routes are often insufficiently marked and are mostly narrow and steep. At times they go over terrain without any paths so that it is es-

*The bus company KTEL operates regular services into many villages on Crete.*

sential to have a good sense of direction. But only very rarely you might need to use your hands. These routes should only be attempted if you are an experienced, sure-footed and fit mountain hiker and do not suffer from vertigo.

## Dangers

Certain sections of exposure, or where it requires the use of the hands, are mentioned in the text.

In some seasons it's possible that you might come across wide areas covered in old snow in the mountain regions over 2000m and here there's a danger of the snow giving way. Snowfields frequently cover fissures and caverns – which are typical at these heights – and streams too. Throughout the year, even in fine weather, there's the possibility of strong winds from the south that can blow over an adult in exposed locations. It is impossible to stand up on the summit in these winds. Between October and May there can be heavy storms in the mountains, which can present particular and unforeseen dangers.

When walking near to villages, isolated farmsteads and outbuildings, you often come across dogs roaming free and sometimes they bark madly and run up to strangers. Bending down, as if to pick a stone up, is usually enough to send them packing.

## Best season

The best conditions for hiking are to be found in the spring and in the autumn – in the months of March, April, May and September, October. Summer is usually too hot, but offers good opportunities for hiking on the Lassíthi plateau and in the Díkti mountains. Winter is often the best time for walking, as there isn't a typical rainy season on Crete.

The thermometer quickly climbs to 20°C as soon as the sun shines, but you should also be prepared for two or three days of rain at a time, as well as thunderstorms and snow above 1000m. As a rule, the frequency of rain and low temperatures decreases from the north-west to the south-east and there are regions on the south coast and in the east where you hardly see a drop of rain all year.

## Equipment

Sturdy footwear made of durable material (because of the many prickly bushes) and with sticky soles, hard-wearing trousers, windproof and waterproof clothing, food, as well as enough fluids and sunscreen, are essential. When visiting monasteries, it is often necessary for women to wear long skirts and to cover their shoulders. Men should wear long trousers.

## Maps

There are not at present any walking maps to a scale of 1:50,000, as is common in central Europe.

Highly recommended are the Harms-ic 1:100,000 maps of Eastern and Western Crete on which the walks in this guide and the E4 route can be found. However, the scale of the maps is insufficient for detailed route finding.

## Walking times
The time details relate to real walking time with a light day-pack and do not include stopping for a rest or to take photos. The length of each stage, the total time, height variations and sometimes the distances too, are given to help you with the route-finding.

## Stops and accommodation
In Crete there are *kafenía* and tavernas almost everywhere, but only in larger tourist places are there restaurants. It is worth taking food with you only on the remote walks, since it is not expensive to stop in the villages for something to eat or drink.

Wild camping is possible on Crete due to the mild climate and is tolerated except in a few instances. However, it is not officially allowed and near to villages and tavernas, you should make use of the usually very cheap rooms, giving some consideration to the often impoverished circumstances of the local inhabitants.

## Access
There is a good improved public bus network. Many of the starting points can be reached by bus very easily, at least in the tourist season. However, at the beginning and the end of the season and during the Greek summer holidays (July/August) you should double check the times in advance on secondary routes.

If you are planning to be off the main roads, hire a car. But the locals will always give you a lift.

## Protection of nature and the environment
Crete still has an extensively unspoiled landscape, at least at first glance, but much has changed in recent years with an increase in tourism and the developments linked with it. The authorities take little action when there are persistent problems concerning the destruction of the landscape, which is caused either by the building of roads, new hotels and holiday complexes, or by tipping rubbish in the open countryside. Even the Cretans themselves demonstrate an amazingly careless attitude to their country.

In spite of the islanders' apparent lack of concern, we would ask you to respect all animal and plant life, to take your rubbish away with you and to be sparing with your use of water.

Never throw cigarette ends away carelessly or light an open fire. There's a very real danger of forest fires on the island, particularly at the height of summer and in the autumn. Be careful also when driving a car. There are few restrictions on the road and so you can come across hire cars in the most unexpected and remote places on the island. And finally, if you see people thoughtlessly destroying the natural surroundings, you might quietly express your surprise.

# Hiking on Crete

## Geography

With a surface area of 8288km² Crete is the largest of all Greek islands and after Sicily, Sardinia, Cyprus and Corsica, the fifth largest in the Mediterranean. It is 260km long and between 12 and 56km wide. The island is dominated by mountains and hill-country and scored by many deep-cut ravines that descend to the sea.

The dominant mountain ranges in the eastern part of the island are as follows: the Díkti mountains (2148m) to the south of the Lassíthi plateau, the Asteroússia mountains (1231m) south of the Messará plain, the Thrípti mountains (1476m) and the Orno mountains (1238m) at Kavoúsi. The coasts in eastern Crete are predominantly rocky, but in between there are inviting bays and beautiful sandy beaches. Package holiday tourism has made its mark on the longer, flat sections of beaches at Hersónissos, Agios Nikólaos and Ierápetra.

A special geological feature is formed by the many limestone plains which are embedded into the mountains. These are the Lassíthi plateau (850m) and the Katharó plateau (1100m). They remain covered in snow right into spring. The melt water from the mountains runs through underground systems into the sea or feeds the few flowing rivers.

The island is watered by many reliable springs which have, in the past, been adequate to supply the island's population. However, increasing tourism and the changeover of agriculture to water-intensive cultivation, are necessitating the investigation of new reservoirs. In so doing, more and more caves are being discovered. Over 3000 of them are already known, but very few of them have been fully explored. The heavy usage of water, especially in the summer months, has already led to an obvious lowering of the water table and the drying-up of some wells in many parts of the island.

## Flora and Fauna

Crete has 1500 species of plants, of which about 10% are only to be found on this island. The types of trees most prevalent are pines, cypress, holm oaks and scarlet oaks, plane trees and eucalyptus.

Vai palm forest at the furthermost point in the north-east is particularly unique. But the appearance of the landscape is largely defined by cultivated trees: olive, orange, lemon, fig, carob, almond and walnut trees. Vineyards are frequently found near to villages and inland.

The tree line is at about 1700m, up to which point there's mainly pastureland with rather sparse vegetation. Herbs thrive here, many of them medicinal. Among them are: sage, thyme, oregano, dittany, rosemary, bay leaf, as well as numerous types of mint. Many kinds of bushes are to be found on the island: oleander, gorse, myrtle, vitex, juniper and many Mediterranean

*The huge 'Pithoi' have been made since Minoan times.*

sclerophyllous plants. Wild flowers bloom in winter and spring: narcissus, cyclamen, anemones, poppies, peonies, daisies, and various types of orchid.

The original Cretan fauna is almost extinct, but you will still find wild goats, eagles, bearded vultures and griffon vultures, all of them protected species. You can also see small animals, rabbits, badgers, turtles, weasels, hedgehogs, snakes and lizards and numerous species of birds.

## Climate and weather
Rainfall is restricted almost totally to the winter months, so that in summer it is mostly dry. The transition periods between these two predominant seasons are accordingly short and often unnoticed. The coldest months are January and February, and the hottest between June and the end of September.

The north is blessed with a somewhat cooler wind in summer, in contrast to the extremely hot south coast. The Sirocco from Africa can be very unpleasant and is often of hurricane force. The temperatures can suddenly increase by 10 degrees and even at night it doesn't get any cooler. Also to be mentioned are the heat storms which occur in the mountains especially. They can be quite violent and occasionally give advance warning of several days of bad weather.

# History of Crete

**6000-2600 BC, Neolithic age:** signs of Neolithic settlement on Crete.

**2600-2000 BC, Pre-Palace era:** migration across the Aegeans onto the plain of central and eastern Crete. Start of working with copper and bronze.

**2000-1700 BC, Old Palace period:** creation of power centres with palaces in Knossos, Malia and Festos. Age of cultural ascendancy. Maritime supremacy of the Minoans. Lively trade with the Aegian islands, Egypt, North Africa and Asia Minor. Upsurge of art and craft.
Development of the 'Linear A' script. Destruction of all sites by an almighty earthquake around 1700 BC.

**1700-1400 BC, New Palace period:** reconstruction of the palaces. Building of the palace at Kato Zakros. High point of art and craft as well as commerce and trade.
'Linear B' script. A volcanic eruption on the island of Santorini around 1450 BC with subsequent earthquakes and seaquakes leads to complete destruction of all palaces and buildings.

**1400-1100 BC, Post Palace period:** Doric invaders from the mainland. Surrender of settlements and slavery of local inhabitants. More basic forms now dominate the craft.

**1100-67 BC, Doric age:** mountain fortresses in Lato, Polirinía, Karfi. Crete becomes part of the Doric settlement. Coins are minted and laws enacted. Trade relations with Phoenix and Egypt. Iron replaces bronze, The 35 states (polis) of Crete feud with one another.

**68 BC-395 AD, Roman era:** Crete becomes a province of Rome with the centre of Gortys on the Messara plain. Stability and peace now prevail on the island. Concession by Rome for the rights of self-government. Age of economic prosperity.
Appearance and spread of Christianity. Following the example of other Roman provinces the building began of roads, bridges, aqueducts, government buildings, temples, theatres, villas and baths.

**395-824 AD, first Byzantine era:** division of the Roman Empire into east and west. Crete is part of the Byzantine (eastern Roman) empire and does not have any special political role to play. Many churches are built during this time.

**824-961 AD, Arab occupation:** under the leadership of Abu Hafs Omar, the Arabs (Saracens) land in 824, conquer Gortys and ravage the whole island. Crete becomes a centre of piracy and slave trade in the eastern Mediterranean.
Byzantine attempts to conquer the island fail.

**961-1204 AD, second Byzantine era:** the Byzantine commander, Nikeophoros, succeeds in driving the Arabs off Crete.
Settling of families from all parts of the Byzantine Empire. Immigrants from Genoa and Venice.

**1204-1669 AD, Venetian era:** in the wake of the 4th crusade Crete falls to Bonifatius II, margrave of Montferrat, who sells it to the Venetians for 10,000 pieces of silver.
In 1206 the Venetians land on Crete with 31 ships, colonise the land according to military bases and give the island a new administrative structure.

**1669-1898, Ottoman Empire:** in spite of great efforts by the Venetians to strengthen their fortification, Hania is conquered in 1645 by the Ottoman fleet. This is followed in 1647 by the capture of Réthimnon and in 1648 begins the siege of Candia (Iráklion) with whose fall in 1669 the Ottoman supremacy is complete.
Crete receives another new administration with the division into legal districts (kazas), each ruled by a *kadi*. Many convert to Islam. In 1821 the Greek mainland rise up against the Ottomans and in 1822 proclaim Greece's independence. Not until 1898, however, do the Ottomans leave the island and Crete receives its independence under an allied high commissioner.

**1898-1913, autonomous government:** the prospect of joining with the motherland gains increasing popularity. In 1913 under Elefterios Venizelos, Crete achieves admission into the Greek state.

**1913-1944, the world wars:** Crete was not involved in the First World War. During the Second World War British troops are sent here from the mainland to keep Crete as a sea base for the British. The Germans land in 1941 and occupy the island until 1944. Many resistance fighters lose their lives.

**1945 to the present day:** after the war many family members have been forced to go abroad to work. Many villages are deserted, and even mainland industry attracts a Cretan workforce.
The gradual rise in agricultural exports since entry into the EU in 1981 and a rapid increase in tourism have resulted in a now continuous upturn in prosperity on the island.

# Information and addresses

## Getting there
– *By air:* charter flights to Iráklion (March to October) are usually the cheapest options. Olympic Airways fly to Athens. There are also cheap charter flights to Athens and from there you can take a plane or ferry to Crete.
– *By ferry:* boats daily from Piraeus (19.00) to Haniá and Iráklion and three times a week to Réthimnon. The crossing takes 11hrs.
– *By car:* from Italy there are ferries from Trieste, Ancona, Ortona, Brindisi, Bari and Otranto to Pátras, sometimes to Iráklion as well.

## Information
*Information on Crete is available from:*
*Great Britain:* Greek National Tourist Organization, 4, Conduit Street, London W1R ODJ, ✆ (0044171) 4994976, 7345997, Fax: 2871369.
*USA:* Greek National Tourist Organization, Olympic Tower 645 Fifth Avenue – New York, NY 10022, ✆ (001212) 4215777, Fax: 8266940

## Telephone
The dialling code for Greece/Crete is 0030. The code from Crete to England is 0044.

## Emergency
There is no mountain rescue service in Crete. In case of emergency notify the nearest police station: police 100 – breakdown 104 – fire service 199.

## Bank Holidays
1st January, 6th January, 25th March, Easter, 1st May, Whitsun, 15th August, 28th October, Christmas.

## Climate
The sun shines 300 days in the year on Crete. What is more, the east is drier than the west. Spring is the most pleasant time for walking. The mild winter lasts three to four months and the coasts are always free of snow. Snow only falls in the mountains and stays until early summer in the highest places.

| CLIMATE TABLE FOR CRETE*) | | | | | | | | | | | | |
|---|---|---|---|---|---|---|---|---|---|---|---|---|
| Month | 1 | 2 | 3 | 4 | 5 | 6 | 7 | 8 | 9 | 10 | 11 | 12 | Year |
| Air °C | 12 | 13 | 14 | 17 | 24 | 24 | 26 | 26 | 24 | 20 | 17 | 14 | 19 |
| Air max. °C | 16 | 16 | 17 | 20 | 24 | 28 | 29 | 29 | 27 | 24 | 21 | 17 | 22 |
| Water °C | 16 | 15 | 16 | 17 | 19 | 22 | 24 | 25 | 24 | 23 | 20 | 17 | 20 |

*) average values

*Seafood composition.*

## Camping

Although, as a rule, wild camping is not allowed in Greece, it's quite possible to put up a tent in the mountains or in isolated bays on Crete. Crete, but you need to be discreet. On the beaches of tourist resorts, on the other hand, there are police controls.

There are over a dozen campsites on the island, but in eastern Crete only in Heraklion, the Lassithi plateau, Hersonissou, Ierapetra and Gourni.

## Sport

Water sports and hiking are the most popular leisure pursuits. The tourist areas also offer surfing, sailing, diving, water skiing, paragliding and mountain biking. You will only find tennis courts in hotel complexes.

## Theft

The times when you could leave your luggage unattended on the beach or elsewhere are gone. Break-ins are rare, but nevertheless, it's advisable not to leave anything valuable in your car.

## Transport on Crete

– *Buses:* the Cretan bus company KTEL maintains an extensive bus network on Crete. It is divided into KTEL Haniá/Réthimnon and KTEL Iráklion/Lassíthi and there's a current timetable available for each. A service runs to larger towns several times a day. There's a regular half-hourly to hourly service on the north coast highway between Iráklion and Agios Nikólaos.
  Buses run far less frequently in the winter.
– *Taxi:* taxis operate with a meter in the towns, but in the country they are called Agoreon and there's a price list.
– *Hire car:* on almost every street corner there are cars and motorbikes for rent.

## Time

The time is two hours later in Greece than in the UK. If it is 12.00 in England, it is 14.00 in Crete.

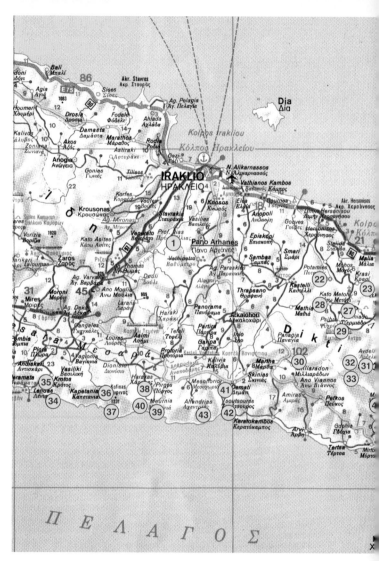

ΠΕΛΑΓΟΣ

# North-east Crete

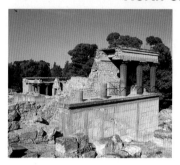

*The palace of Knossós: impressive evidence of the Minoan period of civilization.*

North-east Crete reaches from the mercurial capital of Iráklion to the palm grove of Vái at the eastern end of the island. Due to a well-constructed coastal road and an excellent bus network the towns and villages along the north coast can easily be reached several times a day. Iráklion, with its international airport, is an ideal starting point for a walking holiday in the east of Crete. The weather in this part of the island is more reliable in the spring and in general the east is drier than the west and plants much further advanced in their growth. The most important Minoan settlements are to be found in this section of the island where there's also a major part of the hotel accommodation. Mirabello gulf at Agios Nikólaos, picturesquely surrounded by mountains, is not unjustly described as the most beautiful section of coast on Crete.

If you take the road leading out of Iráklion to the south-east, it is a 7km drive to Knossós. The world famous palace of King Minos and his architect Daidalos was discovered and excavated by the English archaeologist Arthur Evans around the turn of the century. Two and a half thousand years before our time the so-called seafaring people founded the first advanced civilisation here on European soil. A visit to the archaeological museum in Iráklion should certainly precede or follow a tour round Knossós, where all the treasures discovered there – frescoes, sarcophaguses, weapons, jewellery and ceramics – are on display.

If you drive along the road from Knossós into the interior of the island it's worth taking a short walk up onto Joúhtas mountain at Arhánes from where you have a wide view of the surrounding countryside that is amongst the most important wine-growing regions on Crete.

Liménas Hersonissou and Mália on the north coast are, together with Agios Nikólaos and Eloúnda, the most tourist developed areas in north-eastern Crete. Away from the typical manifestations of mass tourism you can find delightful walks in the hinterland, for example onto the Lassíthi plateau, or hikes around the Mirabello gulf at Eloúnda and Kritsá. Excursion boats from Agios Nikólaos also go to the former Venetian fortified island of Spinalónga.

*Vritomartes taverna by the small fishing harbour of Eloúnda.*

One of the scenically most beautiful excavation sites is the Doric fortress of Lató at Kritsá, built out of massive blocks of stone. Not far from there is Panagía-Kerá church with its well-preserved frescoes from the early 14th century. If Creta's gorges appeal to you then you should not miss out on a hike into Kritsá gorge.

At Pahía Ammos you come to the narrowest part of Crete. There's only 12km between the north and south coasts here. You can look down on both seas if you make the ascent of Aféndis Stavroménos, 1476m. It's a beautiful drive from Kavoúsi via the Thrípti meadows onto the summit above. The road twists and turns from Pahía Ammos along the foothills of the Orno mountains going down to the sea to the port of Sitía in the east whose houses lie on the hillside like an amphitheatre around the gulf of the same name.

Sitía is the starting point for the barren east of the island, to the palm forest of Vaí, Toploú monastery or one of the most beautiful beaches on Crete – on the left and right of the table mountain of Palékastro. You can get to another beach at Karoúmes bay, on the other hand, only along a footpath.

Also not to be forgotten is a walk through the 'Grand Canyon' of Crete, the valley of the dead, at the end of which is situated the archaeological site of the Minoan palace at Káto Zákros.

# 1 Onto Joúhtas, 811m

The stone face of Zeus

## Arhánes – Joúhtas – Arhánes

**Starting point:** Arhánes (16km from Iráklion).
**Walking times:** Arhánes – summit 1 hr., return 1 hr.; total time 2 hrs.
**Difference in height:** 400m.

**Grade:** easy walk.
**Stops and accommodation:** tavernas in Arhánes, hotels in Iráklion.
**Bus connections:** Iráklion – Arhánes every hour.

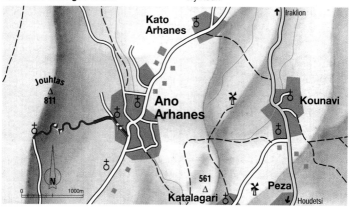

Take the bus in Iráklion that passes the world famous archaeological site of Knossós and after 16km arrives at the little town of Arhánes with its 3500 inhabitants, known as the centre of Cretan wine growing. The desolate looking winepress houses and the rusty wine tanks at the edge of the village are definitely not the best advert for Cretan wine.

Century-old pieces of evidence of Minoan civilization have been brought to light around Arhánes. The Greek archaeologist Jánnis Sakellarákis, who concentrated his excavations to the area around Arhánes, has made a special name for himself. He discovered amongst other things the temple of Anemospília, at the foot of Joúhtas, where a human sacrifice took place thousands of years previously when the whole temple was buried by an earthquake.

Other excavations are the Minoan necropolis and the Minoan manor house in Vathípetrou. On the summit of Joúhtas they discovered a Minoan summit shrine during excavations. Folklore has it that the silhouette of the mountain represents the recumbent face of the god Zeus.

*From the summit of Joúhtas you can enjoy an extensive panorama.*

From the top of the 811m high solitary standing mountain you can enjoy an extensive panorama: the Ida massif and the Kouloúkonas mountains in the west and the mountains of Lassíthi in the east, the sea of houses of Iráklion 10km away on the north coast and the many vineyards around the foot of the mountain.

In the main square in **Arhánes** go along the street past the O.T.E. (bus stop) and take the first lane to the left (Odos Panagioti K. Elenis) as far as a large ochre-coloured building (high school). Go round this to the right past a little old church (Odos Isidórou). The path now becomes a gravel road. At a fork keep left and then immediately right, straight up a concrete track, after some sheds go left up the southern mountain slope.

You will notice the aromatic smell as you make your way through the many different plants growing at the side of the path, particularly in spring. Time and again as you look back there's a view of the tightly packed houses of Arhánes.

Cross over the roadway that leads to the top before coming to the **chapel of Aféndi Christoú Metamórfosi**. Every year on the 6th to 8th August a large pilgrimage takes place onto the summit of the mountain. The excavation site of the Minoan shrine in the north of the summit ridge is unfortunately fenced off. There's also a transmitter mast here. Fenced, newly planted forest areas lie to the south.

# 2  Round walk over Agios Ioánnis cape

Picture book view across Crete's most beautiful gulf

## Pláka – windmills – Agios Ioánnis – windmills – Pláka

**Starting point:** bus stop in Pláka.
**Walking times:** Pláka – windmills 40 mins., windmills – Agios Ioánnis 1¼ hrs., Agios Ioánnis – windmills 1 hr., windmills – Pláka ½ hr.; total time 3½ hrs.
**Difference in height:** 300m.
**Grade:** not a difficult walk, but with a steep ascent at the start. Sturdy shoes, long trousers, drinking water.
**Bus connections:** six times daily in the tourist season Eloúnda – Pláka.
**Stops and accommodation:** tavernas and rooms in Pláka.
**Alternative:** along the gravel road which starts at the northern end of Pláka before the sign for the end of the village and runs parallel to the sea, you come to the little church of Agios Ioánnis, although the views are less spectacular than on the described walk.

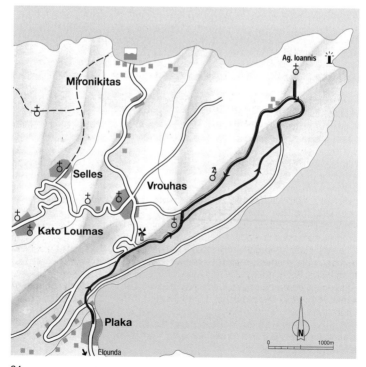

*View of the Mirabello gulf, the fortified island of Spinalónga and Pláka.*

Beyond the peaceful town of Pláka with its beautiful pebble beach, unspoiled villages offer the other face of Crete.

From the bus stop in **Pláka** continue along the road with the pebble beach on your right. At a left-hand bend at the end of the town a gravel path branches off right before the sign for the end of town. The path forks at three chapel-like buildings. Take the left-hand mule path leading uphill and below you can see the excursion boats circling round the island of Spinalónga. After 25 minutes you come to the tarmac road. Stay for about 300m on this and follow it to the first hairpin bend where you take the gravel path uphill until you meet another tarmac road. After 5 minutes you will see windmills ahead and a **little church**.

A concrete track branches off to the right in front of this. At a trig point you will experience the most beautiful view across the Mirabello gulf with the Thrípti mountains on the horizon and Aféndis Stavroménos. Stay on the concrete track which goes beside a telephone line, past a chapel, towards a hilltop. From the chapel follow the concrete track for about another 250m until a narrow path turns off right before a left-hand bend (large cairn). This leads slightly downhill between dry stonewalls. Far below you can see the shimmering turquoise-blue sea.

The very overgrown path continues through gorse bushes in the same direction and then meets a gravel road which slowly ascends along the coast from Pláka. Follow the gravel road which runs uphill round a left-hand bend. After a right-hand bend above a gorge, a gravel path leads to the **chapel of Agios Ioánnis** above the cape of the same name. The view extends into the distance along the coastline.

Return to the gravel road and keep straight on towards the transmitter ahead. This brings you back to the tarmac road at the windmills. Now return to **Pláka** the way you came.

# 3   From Eloúnda to Pláka

Windmills above the Mirabello gulf

## Eloúnda – Pinés – Havgás – Pláka

*A well on the beach of Pláka.*

**Starting point:** centre of Eloúnda.
**Walking times:** Eloúnda – Pinés ¾ hr., Pinés – Havgás 1¼ hrs., Havgás – Pláka ¾ hr.; total time 2¾ hrs.
**Difference in height:** 330m.
**Grade:** not a difficult walk, but with some ascents and fabulous views as a compensation. Good footwear, drinking water.
**Bus connections:** hourly Agios Nikólaos – Eloúnda, hourly Eloúnda – Pláka in the tourist season.
**Stops and accommodation:** tavernas and rooms in Eloúnda and Pláka.

In the centre of **Eloúnda**, at the bus stop in the square, follow the road that goes past on the left of the church and the clock tower. After 8 minutes a signpost indicates right to the village of Mavrikianó. Go straight ahead. A minute later you pass the village sign of Káto Eloúnda. As you continue you can see the village of Páno Eloúnda ahead (upper Eloúnda).

After the sign for Páno Eloúnda turn left onto a concrete road that runs between stonewalls. After an underpass go up into the village on the right. Past a *kafeníon* you branch off at the first road, follow this straight on through the village and go left at the northern end of the village uphill along a concrete path which brings you to the tarmac road again. Cross over this and ascend a mule path opposite. After 3 minutes cross over the road again. The paved path continues uphill between dry stonewalls until it meets a broader gravel path. Turn left onto this and you soon reach a ridge with several old **windmills**.

Descend the concrete path to the tarmac road and on the right you can see a round threshing floor. The path crosses the tarmac road and leads straight on past some houses of the village of **Pinés** which lies in the midst of olive, almond and carob trees. The concrete path soon turns to the right. Go straight on along the paved path. After 3 minutes turn right – up between high dry stonewalls – for a short way on a gravel path until the dry stonewall path continues left to the tarmac road. Follow this to the right until it descends to a sign for a bend. Now turn left up a concrete path bordered by dry stonewalls, after a minute go left behind a gate and shortly after that go right at another fork. The path then descends again. You meet a roadway where you go left and after 2 minutes turn right along a gravel road down into a hollow. At the first turn-off to the left make your way towards a distinct wire fence. Then continue right between two wire fences. After a minute you walk beneath the shady covering of an oak tree. Continue straight on beside the left-hand wire fence.

The narrow path starts to descend slightly and then goes up between gorse and sage bushes and after a swing to the right it ascends gradually up between dry stonewalls until you turn right onto the road to Plaka. You are soon afforded an impressive view down a gorge to the island of Spinalónga. Before that you can see the village of **Havgás** on a mountain ridge. Follow the road past the houses to Pláka.

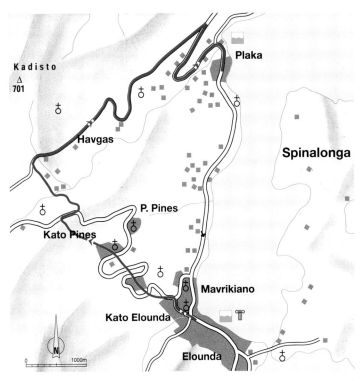

# 4 From Agios Nikólaos to Lató

To the Doric mountain fortress built in an impressive location

## Agios Nikólaos – Hamiló – Lató – Kritsá

**Starting point:** Hamiló, 6km west of Agios Nikólaos (by taxi).
**Walking times:** Hamiló – Lató 1 hr., Lató – Kritsá 1 hr.; total time 2 hrs.
**Difference in height:** 200m.
**Grade:** not a difficult walk. Do not forget sun protection.
**Stops and accommodation:** tavernas and rooms in Agios Nikólaos and Kritsá.
**Bus connections:** frequent bus service Agios Nikólaos – Kritsá.
**Alternative:** continue along the path to Panagía-Kéra church and to Kritsá.

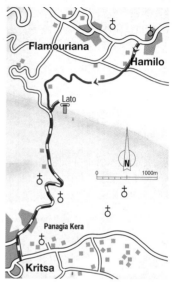

Agios Nikólaos and its surrounding area are a good starting point for some scenically delightful walks. One of them leads to the Doric settlement of Lató from the 8th century BC, whose location has beautiful views. Most of the ruins, however, date back to the 4th and 3rd century BC when it was a boom town in the Minoan period. The settlement was discovered by the English archaeologist Evans, who also discovered Knossós.

Begin the walk in the village of **Hamiló**, 4.5km from Agios Nikólaos. 50m beyond the village, at a rusty signpost, leave the road along a track to the left between olive groves. Ignore all turn-offs. After 20 minutes you come to a new building. 100m further on the path joins a roadway between a dry streambed and a stonewall which you follow along to the left. A few minutes later turn left onto a gravel road which you leave again to the left after 30m (*red waymarker arrow on stone*).

The path forks 50 metres further on: left goes to a house, but you follow the narrow footpath to the right through two gates and soon turns out to be a formerly paved path. After ascending for half an hour up the hillside, at a *Ikonostasi* (wayside shrine) you meet the road coming from Kritsá.

Turn left onto this and go another 10 minutes uphill until you reach the entrance gate to the Doric settlement of Lató. You get an immediate impres-

*View of the ruins of Lató.*

sion of the huge square-cut stones stacked up to form the walls. There are similarities in the building style with the walls of Mykene and Tiryns, and they even have something in common with the Inca buildings in Peru so that we are not disinclined to calling Lató the 'Maccu Piccu' of Crete. In any case you should definitely climb up to the upper rocks. From there you can enjoy a wide view across the Mirabello gulf and Agios Nikólaos in the distance, as well as a good overview of the ruins lying below.

**Continuing to Kritsá and the Panagía-Kéra church:** follow the gravel road downhill to Lató, through olive and almond trees, until you come to the tarmac road to Kritsá. If you turn right here you will reach the village of Kritsá – left (in the direction Agios Nikólaos) continues for a little more than 1 km to the famous Byzantine Panagía-Kéra church dating from the 14<sup>th</sup> century.

# 5  Through the Kritsá gorge to Tápes

Imposing gorge away from the hoards of tourists

### Kritsá – Tápes – Kritsá

**Starting point:** road to Lató at the start of the village of Kritsá.
**Walking times:** Kritsá – Tápes 2¼ hrs., Tápes – Kritsá 1¾ hrs.; total time 4 hrs.
**Difference in height:** 275m.
**Grade:** only possible when the streambed is dry. Sun protection, water and provisions.
**Bus connections:** frequent bus service Agios Nikólaos – Kritsá, daily at 14.30 Tápes – Agios Nikólaos.
**Stops and accommodation:** tavernas and rooms in Agios Nikólaos and Kritsá, *kafeníon* in Tápes.

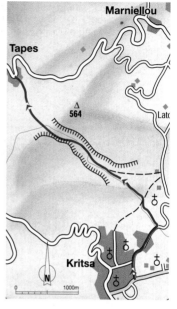

At the lower end of **Kritsá** village go along the road to Lató, and at a bridge you reach the riverbed which emerges out of the gorge walls that you can see ahead. Either descend immediately here down to the riverbed or go left after the bridge along a track (400m). When the track bends to the right after 15 minutes, go down left to the riverbed.

Continue along the bottom of the gorge over rocks and boulders where you also need to use your hands at times. After 25 minutes a wire fence bars your way along the gorge. 5m above there's a gate which you can walk through. After 35 minutes you come to another gate. The gorge walls are now getting closer and closer together, shaped and polished by the masses of water that rushes through. It seems almost impossible that you will be able to get through here without any difficulty.

After 55 minutes there's a fork in the gorge. Take the right-hand branch following a fence. Five minutes later you walk across a fence that has been trampled down. After another 10 minutes you have to climb over another fence (no problem). After that the terrain opens out. Keep in the streambed until, after a good 1¼ hours, an insurmountable fence bars your path along the streambed. At this point keep right for 150m uphill, go through an iron gate and then it's a scramble down again to the streambed. After two hours walking you can now see the houses of Tápes in the distance. There's a fork in the riverbed. On the right above the gravelly bed of the stream there's a track, running next to the narrower right-hand branch, which then crosses over to the other side at a ford.

After 25m a path leads up left to **Tápes** (take note of the cairns). The path comes out directly by the small *kafeníon*, O Prinos, which is on the road where the bus to Agios Nikólaos also stops. The owner is keen to serve you, but be careful – he charges double the normal prices.

Return to Kritsá either through the gorge or as in Walk 26, above the gorge on the north side.

*In the Kritsá gorge.*

# 6    From Mardáti to Istron

Panoramic walk above the Mirabello gulf

## Agios Nikólaos – Mardáti – Kroústas – Istron

**Starting point:** bus station in Agios Nikólaos.
**Walking times:** Mardáti – Kroústas 1¼ hrs., Kroústas – Istron 2¾ hrs.; total time 4 hrs.
**Difference in height:** ascent 390m, descent 540m.
**Grade:** not a difficult walk, but a rather

strenuous ascent and long descent. Good footwear, sun protection, water.
**Bus connections:** frequent bus service from Agios Nikólaos to Mardáti (Kritsá) and Istron – Agios Nikólaos each taking about 1½ hrs.
**Stops and accommodation:** tavernas in Kroústas and Istron, rooms in Istron.

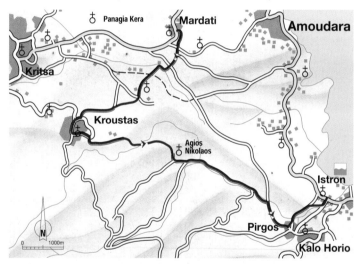

On this walk not far away from the hustle and bustle of Agios Nikólaos and Eloúnda you can get to know the unspoiled Greek landscape around the Mirabello gulf and enjoy its unique panoramic character.

The starting point for this walk is the **bus station in Agios Nikólaos**. Take one of the frequent buses to Kritsá, but get off in **Mardáti** after 10 minutes. From the bus stop (opposite the Mardáti taverna) follow the tarmac road to Kritsá. After 5 minutes (250m) turn left beyond the village exit sign onto a track. After two minutes you meet another roadway. Go left here and immediately right. Ignore a turn-off to the left shortly afterwards and carry straight

*The south-eastern end of the village of Kritsá.*

on. After 12 minutes you come to a crossroads. Turn left and 50m further on, to the right again. You come to a **streambed**, go up along this as it swings to the right.

At a little house with a long bower of vines and gourds leave the riverbed to the left and climb up along the roadway. The view opens up on the right of the village of Kritsá lying on the hillside. A little later go between the ruins of two windmills. Carry straight on along the roadway and on the slope ahead you can see the white-washed chapel of Agios Apóstoli.

At a fork take the right-hand ascending branch of the roadway which leads past the chapel just above it. Go straight across a crossroads. It continues steeply uphill where the path narrows, and on the right-hand side you go past a water basin from where there's a beautiful view back to Agios Nikólaos. The path leads up further through cistus and oregano bushes. After 50 minutes you meet a roadway from where you get another view over to Kritsá and in the distance beyond, Tápes. Swing left onto the roadway and you become aware of the unique panoramic character of this walk. Still following this path, you arrive in **Kroústas**. At a circular roadway junction go left and find your way through the narrow streets of the village until you meet the tarmac road to Kritsá. There's one *kafenίon* after another along the main road that is lined with mulberry trees.

Continue your walk along this road to the left as far as the **church**. Go left here across the yard and down the little village street until you are leaving Kroústas in a south-easterly direction along a descending concrete path. You will know if you're on the right path if you come past a house with a white plastic door. The path is heading in the exact direction of the isthmus at Istron. On the left-hand side you can see the houses of Kroústas above sloping rock faces. The path leaves the village parallel to the path you came on, separated by a gorge.

After 5 minutes the roadway makes a turn where a descending mule path begins and then immediately meets the gravel road again. Twenty minutes after Kroústas, take the descending path to the right (cairn). The path runs down into the left-hand side of a gorge and back up to the top on the other

*After Kroústas, it's a steady downhill walk to Istron.*

*The kafeníon under shady mulberry trees in Kroústas.*

side. Some red waymarkers reassure you that you are on the right path. Ascend another 50 vertical metres before then heading continuously downhill. After over an hour from Kroústas you reach the **little church of Agios Nikólaos**. From here continue descending the roadway. Ignore a turn-off that follows immediately to the right.

After 10 minutes the roadway swings over to the right-hand side of the valley and continues through olive groves. Half an hour after the little church a roadway joins from the right. Continue down to the left on the right-hand side of the riverbed. After just under ¾ hour (from the little church) Kalo Hório emerges on the hillside ahead. At a turn-off shortly before an electricity pylon, go straight ahead, not left. A minute later along a gravel roadway change over onto the left-hand side of the riverbed. After about 2 hours you meet the main road from Agios Nikólaos to Sitía in **Istron**. Follow the road to the right over the bridge and 200m further on you come to the bus stop at the Levka taverna.

# 7 To the monastery of Faneroménis built in the rock

A box seat above the gulf of Mirabello

## Gourniá – Moni Faneroménis – Gourniá

**Starting point:** Gourniá Moon campsite on the road Agios Nikólaos – Sitía, 3km west of Pahía Ammos.

**Walking times:** road – monastery 2 hrs., monastery – transmitter 30 mins., descent to the road 1½ hrs.; total time 4 hrs.

**Difference in height:** 600m.

**Grade:** easy walk on good paths, mostly concrete or gravel, narrow road. No shade, very hot in summer.

**Stops and accommodation:** in nearby Agios Nikólaos and along the whole coastline there's a large number of rooms for rent in all categories.

**Bus connections:** several busses a day from Agios Nikólaos to Sitía and in the opposite direction. Busses stop at the campsite if you are waiting.

**Tip:** a trip to Gourniá, the largest and most important excavated Minoan town on Crete.

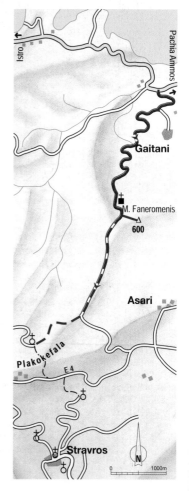

If you visit the ancient site of Gourniá, you should make the time for a walk to the monastery.

3km west of Gourniá, opposite the **Gourniá Moon campsite**, a sign indicates the road leading steeply uphill. The road, concreted almost all the way, zigzags up the slope. It is also possible to drive up here. On less warm days, though, it's nice to do this section on foot.

The 6km long road leads past several mountain huts through the windswept and weather-beaten landscape, and there is a fantastic view down to the gulf of Mirabello

*The church in the cave, the oldest part of Faneroménis monastery.*

all the way. After about 2 hours you have gained 550 vertical metres and after a bend you can see ahead, quite unexpectedly, the large fortified monastery that is built close to a rock face. From the various terraces of the monastery there's a wide view across the deeply cut valley north-westwards to the white line of houses of Agios Nikólaos. The monastery has water provided from a spring and a large guesthouse.

The story goes that in 1170 an icon of the Virgin Mary was found up here in a cave. From that moment on they began to build first a church in a cave at this legendary spot, and then gradually the monastery. A monk still lives here, but every year on 15th August, at the festival of Panagía, a big festival takes place up here.

The gravel road goes past the monastery for another 1km up onto the 600m high hill and leads as far as the nearby **transmitter** from where you have a fabulous panoramic view.

Go back the same way. If you follow the gravel road to the right at the fork just before the transmitter, after about an hour you will reach the **chapel** you can see in the distance on Plakokéfala. From there you can continue walking in the direction of Stavrós (Walk 48) or Messeléri (Walk 47). There and back from the chapel, 2-2½ hrs.

# 8   From Vasilikí to Episkopí

Walk between the seas

## Vasilikí – Asarí – Episkopí

**Starting point:** village square in Vasilikí.
**Walking times:** Vasilikí – Asarí 2 hrs., Asarí – Episkopí 2¼ hrs.; total time 4¼ hrs.
**Difference in height:** ascent 340m, descent 330m.
**Grade:** not a difficult walk, but a long one on roadways. Sun protection, provisions and drinking water.
**Bus connections:** every one to two hours Agios Nikólaos – Vasilikí – Episkopí – Ierápetra.
**Stops and accommodation:** *kafeníon* in Vasilikí, taverna in Episkopí. Rooms in Agios Nikólaos, Ierápetra, Pahía Ammos.

In the first section of this walk you can enjoy beautiful views of the Cretan Sea on the north side of the island and in the second part, the Libyan Sea in the south.

The walk begins at the village square in **Vasilikí**. Not every bus between Agios Nikólaos – Ierápetra goes up into the village. If you get out on the main road, it's a 15-minute walk to Vasilikí.

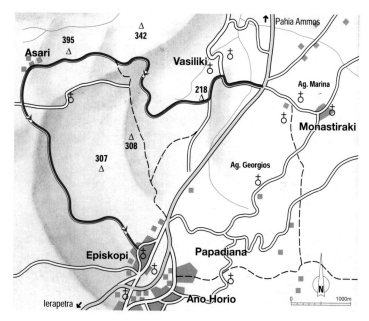

In Vasilikí take the road which goes uphill opposite the kiosk. On this road take the third turning off to the left (telephone mast, small hydrant). At the uppermost houses you then meet a concrete path that runs due south. Fifteen minutes later the roadway forks. Carry straight on, do not turn left! Three minutes later, at a fork, go straight on up the hill. Ignore a second turning off to the right. You can see Aféndis Stavroménos up on the left in the background above the V-cleft of the Monastiráki gorge. The main path makes a long loop round to the right, from where you have another good view back to Vasilikí, and below a cave, continues northwards in the direction of the island of Psíra. Before the road swings round to the south again on a left-hand bend after the mountain, you have a wonderful view of the beach at Pahía Ammos and the little islands lying off the coast. As you continue along the path you can see the houses in the distance of Agios Nikólaos. At the upper end of the gorge that drops down to the sea, the road goes round a right-hand bend and after another left-hand bend leads into a valley.

At a twin-trunked olive tree, the first of four olive trees, continue along the roadway (left) which now ascends again. A strangely dramatic, rugged landscape now surrounds you. The road forks 10 minutes after the olive trees. Take the left branch. You then meet another fork where you go left. At another fork a bit later on you keep right.

*The Byzantine church in Episkopí.*

Soon after that the path swings to the east. You now have a fantastic view of the sea and Ierápetra. You eventually walk over a mountain ridge that allows you a view of Káto Horió opposite. Further on you can take a shortcut from the long left-hand bend in the roadway, along a clearly visible path. The track joins a tarmac road to Ierápetra, 300m before the place name sign of **Episkopí**.

The bus stop is to be found below the village square where there's also a taverna. Do not miss the Byzantine church from the 12/13th century that stands just below the road.

# 9  From Kavoúsi onto Thriptí

Alpine ascent with rewarding views

## Kavoúsi – Thriptí meadows – Monastiráki and Káto Horió

**Starting point:** Kavoúsi.
**Walking times:** Kavoúsi – Thriptí 2¾ hrs.,
Thriptí – Monastiráki 3 hrs. or Thriptí – Káto
Horió 3½ hrs.; total time 5¾ or 6¼ hrs.
**Difference in height:** 700m.
**Grade:** demanding mountain walk requir-
ing a good level of firness. Provisions, sun
protection.
Some route-finding is needed for the de-
scent to Monastiráki.

**Bus connections:** eight buses a day to
Kavoúsi on the main line between Agios
Nikólaos – Sitía in the tourist season.
Monastiráki and Káto Horió both lie 2 km
off the main bus route to Ierápetra: ten
times daily in the tourist season.
**Stops and accommodation:** tavernas in
Kavoúsi and Káto Horió.
*Kafeníon* at Thriptí in the summer. Rooms
in Kavoúsi.

Your starting point in **Kavoúsi** lies
on the coastal road from Agios
Nikólaos to Sitía, 5km after Pahía
Ammos. The path begins behind
the church and leads along the village street to the south as far as a
kiosk. Turn left here into Odos
Moutsáki. Then turn right into the
next tiny street called Odos
Dermitsáki and up to the south end
of the village. Turning right past a
small church and a well and along a
water channel take a broad paved
path uphill. As you glance back
there's an enchanting view of the
shimmering Mirabello gulf.
After about 1½ hours the path forks

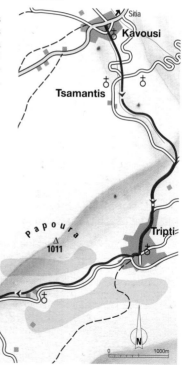

*The old mule path from Kavoúsi onto the Thripti meadows.*

and you follow the waymarkers to the left. After two hours you reach a **pass** (820m), after which you can see the massive rock of Aféndis Stavroménos. Follow the footpath again to the left until you come to a turning off to the right before the first stone buildings. It goes for a short way uphill at first and five minutes later you cross over a roadway and through a valley cleft to reach the first houses of **Thriptí**. (If you now want to climb Aféndis Stavroménos, carry straight on at the first fork in the roadway. Your objective is the highest house below the edge of the wood. See Walk 11).

**Path from Thriptí to Monastiráki:** the roadway to Káto Horió begins at the western end of Thriptí (3½ hour walk). After only a minute you leave the roadway at a little house below a **telephone pole** and via a hollow running downhill reach the other slope.

After 5 minutes the path goes between **water houses**, then descends along a roadway on the left side of the gorge through a pine forest. Go right at a fork (little houses and orchards). After an hour you can see the cleft of the Monastiráki gorge ahead. Shortly after that you come across the **little church of Agia Anna** at the side of the path. 50m further on take the right-hand fork and 5 minutes later, at another fork, go again to the right (concrete plinth). Cross over a narrow streambed then make a short ascent and the view opens out. Terracing of the terrain makes route-finding difficult. Look for the path to the left on the *lower terraces*! You also need to be careful as you descend the stony path by the oleander bushes. Go right here and at the following fork. The narrow path eventually reaches a track that joins the road to Pahía Ammos.

# 10 Onto Aféndis Stavroménos, 1476m

Between the seas

## Thriptí – Aféndis Stavroménos – Thriptí

**Starting point:** Thriptí, easy to reach on foot, see Walk 9, or by car from Káto Horió.
**Walking times:** Thriptí – Aféndis Stavroménos 1¾ hrs., Aféndis Stavroménos – Thriptí 1¼ hrs.; total time 3 hrs.

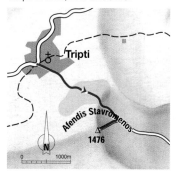

**Difference in height:** 700m.
**Grade:** rewarding mountain walk with fantastic views. Good footwear, sun protection, drinking water.
**Bus connections:** eight times daily to Kavoúsi on the main line bus between Agios Nikólaos – Sitía in the tourist season. Monastiráki and Káto Horió each lie 2km off the main bus route to Ierápetra: ten a day in the tourist season.
**Stops and accommodation:** tavernas in Kavoúsi and Káto Horió. There's a *kafeníon* open on Thrípti in the summer. Otherwise, rooms in Kavoúsi. Possibility of staying overnight on Thriptí by arrangement.
**Alternatives:** a climb from Kavoúsi to Thriptí is worth it simply for the delightful views down the mountain. The ascent and descent of Aféndis Stavroménos is also possible from the south coast from Shinokapsala.

Not everyone can summon up the energy to climb Aféndis Stavroménos after the long ascent from Kavoúsi to Thriptí. So for these hikers it's possible to drive by car from **Kato Horió** up to **Thriptí**. The condition of the gravel road, however, requires a more robust kind of car.

If you drive from the western end of the village along the road from Kato Horió you come to a car park with a water trough. A gravel road from here leads to the houses at the eastern edge of the mountainside. After about five minutes a red marked path turns off steeply uphill and leads to the highest house below the edge of the forest. The path has become more and more overgrown in the last few years, but there is roadway now going up to the highest house, which is a lot easier. Continue up steeply through pine forest. Various types of small orchids are widespread here.

After the forest boundary you climb over scree and rock further uphill (well-marked). It gets flatter afterwards, goes across a small plain where you meet a roadway which has been built from the other side. The waymarked path has been destroyed by building work. Continue your way along the road that finally brings you to the summit of **Aféndis Stavroménos**. There's a white-washed chapel on the top where, every year on 14th September, they celebrate the anniversary of the church's foundation. The mountain farmers from the surrounding area stay the night there and the following day is spent celebrating mass, eating, drinking and dancing.

Those who achieve the huge feat of climbing from Kavoúsi onto the summit – it's a good 1400 vertical metres – are rewarded with far-reaching views. Below you lies the narrowest part of Crete where the contours of the north and south coasts come closer together. The views reach as far as the south-eastern end of Crete with the off-shore island of Koufoníssi in the Libyan Sea and across the whole of the Mirabello gulf with Agios Nikólaos and Spinalónga in the north. To the west you can see the Díkti mountains closing off the Lassíthi plateau to the south.

*On the summit of Aféndis Stavroménos.*

# 11 From Kavoúsi to Melísses

Along mule paths into the Orno mountains

**Kavoúsi – Melísses – Kavoúsi**

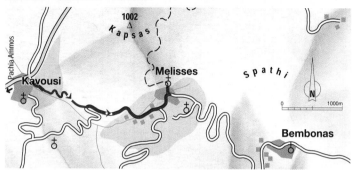

**Starting point:** Kavoúsi, 27km east of Agios Nikólaos, on the main highway towards Sitía.

**Walking times:** Kavoúsi – start of the gorge 20 mins., mule path – road 45 mins., road – Melísses 45 mins., descent 1¼ hrs.; total time 3-3½ hrs.

**Difference in height:** ascent 600m, descent 600m.

**Grade:** easy mountain walk along good paths. Shade in places, also possible in summer.

**Bus connections:** several a day from Agios Nikólaos – Sitía and the reverse.

**Stops and accommodation:** tavernas and rooms in Kavoúsi, numerous overnight possibilities along the main road to Agios Nikólaos.

A short, but very rewarding walk leads from **Kavoúsi** into the mountain village of Melísses situated in the Orno mountains. The still fairly unspoiled village lies directly at the foot of the steep rock face of the 1002m Kapsás.

At the eastern end of the village there's a gravel road branching off from the main road which leads towards the well visible gorge. Go left at the first turn-off following a dry streambed and the road ends immediately before the sheer drop into the gorge. The gorge itself is not passable. About 100m before the end of the road the gravel road crosses the pebbly streambed and this is where the old paved mule path clearly starts. It zigzags steadily up the steep slope and way above the gorge, crosses over the left side into the valley. The old well-laid path is still in good condition and winds up the steep rough terrain. After a good hour the paved path comes to an end and you meet the gravel road coming up from the gorge.

Follow this further uphill. The path keeps on the left-hand side up the valley until after 15 minutes you reach the first huts of **Melísses**. The village with

*The landscape of the Orno mountains.*

several chapels sprawls out across the very green valley and the highest houses are to be found at an altitude of almost 700m. At the first fork in the road go left uphill and come to the **chapel** which you have been able to see for a long time. It lies on a small hill above the newly renovated houses and ruins. A shady place to sit and gaze around with a wide, green valley basin spreading out below!

# 12 From Lástros to Melísses

Along old paths into the Orno mountains

### Lástros – Orno mountains – Melísses (Kavoúsi)

**Starting point:** Lástros, 350m, at the eastern side of the steep Kapsás mountain, on the road from Agios Nikólaos to Sitía.
**Walking times:** Lástros – roadway 45 mins., roadway – col 1 hr., col – Melísses 45 mins.; total time 2½-3 hrs.
**Difference in height:** ascent 300m, descent as far as Melísses 200m, to Kavoúsi 600m.

**Grade:** easy on the ascent, but a tough and strenuous walk on the descent along little-used paths and in some places bad paths. Good footwear essential.
**Stops and accommodation:** tavernas and rooms in Kavoúsi and along the road to Agios Nikólaos.
**Bus connections:** several daily Agios Nikólaos – Sitía.

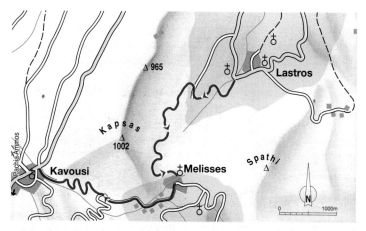

Coming from Agios Nikólaos the road ascends to Kavoúsi steeply up the west side of Kapsás and goes round the conical mountain. On the east side, at an altitude of 350m, lies the little village of **Lástros.**

From the village go back to the main road and carry on for another 500m in the direction of Agios Nikólaos. The road crosses the valley bottom round a narrow right-hand bend. Before the bridge on the side of the mountain, at the crash barrier, a narrow path leads down into the dry streambed. At the bottom you meet an old paved footpath that you follow uphill. Passing an old cistern filled with water the path ascends in the shade. The path leaves the streambed for a short while to the left, but then bends back towards it to eventually lead up the slope to the right as a broad paved path.

*The idyllically situated Lástros at the edge of the Orno mountains.*

After a total of 45 minutes you reach a broad gravel road which you take to the right. After about 100m the old path continues to the left uphill. It goes round a wide loop to the right, at the edge of the drop, uphill beside enormous agaves towards the massif in the west. The luxuriant orchards of at first orange and lemon trees and vegetable plants now give way to olive trees and the higher you climb, the more barren the land becomes. At an altitude of 520m the path crosses a gorge running up to the right and you have to climb over a pasture fence. The paved path keeps to the right-hand side of the valley below Kapsás mountain towards the open, 650m high col to the right of Spathí mountain.

From the col descend in a southerly direction over the right side of the valley. There are now only tracks here, but they are easy to follow. Walk downhill keeping on the right-hand slope. It's impossible to descend the valley cleft directly because it is too steep and overgrown. Descend steeply across old terraces towards a rib of rock running down from above and along the now distinct path you come to some ruins. The path leads on the left of these downhill across a slope to the left, then almost on the level through the small side valley towards the ruins and houses opposite with the white church you have been able to see from a long way off.

Directly below the house ruins go past a vineyard bordered with stones to the first house and the road running along behind it. Walk along this road through the deserted looking village of **Melísses** in 1¼ hours down to **Kavoúsi** (see Walk 11).

# 13 From Móhlos to Sfáka

A round walk out of the Minoan port of Móhlos

### Móhlos – Sfáka – Móhlos

**Starting point:** Móhlos, 6.5km below the village of Sfáka, in a bay. The island of Móhlos lies opposite.

**Walking times:** Móhlos – turn-off along a track 30 mins., turn-off – tarmac road 50 mins., tarmac road – Sfáka 10 mins., Sfáka – start of the streambed 45 mins., through the gorge 30 mins., road – Móhlos 15 mins.; total time 3 hrs.

**Difference in height:** ascent 300m, descent 300m.

**Grade:** easy walk, in places along the pebbly streambed on the descent. Partly shaded, very hot in summer, best time of the day in the afternoon.

**Stops and accommodation:** tavernas, rooms, hotels in and around Móhlos.

**Bus connections:** bus stop in Sfáka, several daily Agios Nikólaos – Sitía, from Sfáka to Móhlos only by taxi.

**Tip:** the island of Móhlos 150m away with excavations of a Minoan settlement. Fishing boats will take you from the harbour to the island on request.

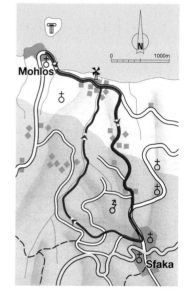

Only a few years ago Móhlos was still a small, almost forgotten fishing village. Situated in a picturesque location in the small bay opposite the island of the same name there is now a lot of new development in the village and surrounding area. Móhlos, however, has not lost its charm. It was of great significance in the Minoan era as the most important port of the north coast, presumably even of the whole island (2600 to 1850 and 1700 to 1550 BC). The many valuable finds are on display in the archaeological museum in Heráklion.

From the centre of the old village at the small harbour in **Móhlos** the road leads out and along beside the sea to the east, through a flat and very fertile coastal strip. Vineyards with terraces planted with olive trees and orchards lie on your right and left. Follow the tarmac road for half an hour. It crosses a small side valley. Passing greenhouses, a modern windmill, many newly built houses and the new Club Hotel a little away from the road, head towards a large side valley which comes down from the right. Fifty metres before it (on the left side of the road there's a large electricity pylon) a *blue arrow* with the letter 'S' (Sfáka) indicates the gravel road coming from the right. The gravel road leads through orchards, past some solitary houses, at first over level ground, later more steeply winding up across the hills in the direction of Sfáka (*blue arrows at junctions*, but they are sometimes rather hidden). After about 30 minutes going uphill the path reaches a flat, narrow ridge top. There's a beautiful view on both sides down into the valleys. On the right above you can see a transmitter. After another 10 minutes, past farmsteads and solitary houses, the gravel road joins the tarmac road between Sfáka – Móhlos (if you are walking in the opposite direction, do not take the gravel road turning off sharply to the left, take the second turn-off left). After the 300 vertical metre ascent, the last few minutes are along the tarmac road on the level into **Sfáka**. You will find several *kafenía* in the small village square where you can stop for a break. The beautifully situated village is divided into two by the road connecting Agios Nikólaos – Sitía. The church, visible form afar, is in the upper part and is well worth a visit and affords the hiker a wonderful view.

From the small village square go down a set of broad steps to the cemetery below. Carry straight on along the concrete path at the first junction (right goes to the cemetery). Just afterwards a gravel road leads left again up to the main road above, but you follow the old footpath further downhill. After a few metres there's a well on your right, just off the path, with several troughs. The luxuriant orchards below the village indicate an abundant water supply and loads of plastic pipes runs off like spiders' webs down into the orchards.

Follow the old, sometimes paved footpath for a bit longer, across an old arched bridge, down into the valley until it comes to an end at a gravel road. Descend the road for a few minutes as far as a solitary olive tree standing almost in the middle of the gravel road. Five metres after it a narrow path leads left downhill across two or three terraces to the streambed further below. At this point you've been walking for three quarters of an hour from the village. The walk now takes you mostly through the gravelly streambed where, now and then, some short stretches of the old path emerge (ignore a gravel road that comes down from above close to the stream). The descent lasts about another half hour through the sometimes narrow, dry stony streambed of the valley that, time and again, is enclosed by small rock faces.

You meet the tarmac road directly by the windmill at the point where the road between Móhlos and Sfáka crossed the first side valley in the first part of your walk, and return to Móhlos in 15 minutes.

# 14 From Sfáka via Plátanos to Tourlotí

The landscape below the Orno mountains

## Sfáka – Plátanos – Tourlotí

**Starting point:** bus stop in Sfáka.
**Walking times:** Sfáka – Plátanos 1¾ hrs.,
Plátanos – Tourlotí 1¾ hrs.; total time
3½ hrs.
**Difference in height:** ascent 535m, descent 430m.
**Grade:** not a difficult walk, but with a long ascent.
Good footwear, sun protection, provisions and water.
**Bus connections:** about every 2 hrs.
Agios Nikólaos – Sitía.
**Stops and accommodation:** *kafenía* in
Sfáka and Tourlotí. Rooms in Agios
Nikólaos, Pahía Ammos and Sitía.

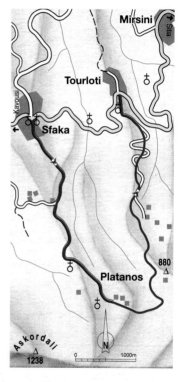

This walk on the southern foothills of the Orno mountains goes mainly along gravel paths. It gives you beautiful views down onto the villages situated on the coastal road to Sitía, and of the Gulf of Móhlos.

Your starting point is the bus stop at the kiosk in **Sfáka**. Behind it you can see some broad, flat steps with a white handrail. Go up these and once you arrive at the top take the road to the right which leads through the upper part of the village. After seven minutes you leave the village along a roadway and after 10 minutes come to a turning off to the left, but you keep on the main path. Three minutes later after a right-hand bend a mule path branches off left from the road. Turn left again after that onto the gravel road. If you look back, you can see your destination of Tourlotí beyond Sfáka.

The gravel road makes a turn to the right through a gorge-like cleft. About 400m further on the old path ascends left again between terraces of vines (rather overgrown). During the ascent the view opens out of the conical peak of Askordaliá (1237m), the highest elevation of the Orno mountains.

*View of Tourlotí. Móhlos on the left with the off-shore island.*

The old path later joins the main path again. You can see terraces of vines opposite with the ruins of a building. At the next bend in the path you can see across to the village of Lástros. As the old path is noticeably overgrown, it's best to walk along the roadway. The ground levels out at the top and at two wild pear trees you come to an inviting spot for a rest with views over the Mirabello gulf.

After an hour a path leads down left to little houses and cattle pens and a new church beyond. But you keep right along the main roadway which ascends gently again. On the right you will see a threshing circle. Carry on along the roadway from where there's a pleasant panoramic view. Ignore a turning off to the left at a wild pear tree and head for the mountains. A little later you come past a threshing circle (left) and through an iron gate. The deep cisterns are worth looking at with the steps going down the walls in a spiral and another peculiarity is the apple trees, which are a rarity in this otherwise so barren landscape. Leave this green oasis through a second gate. The roadway now runs on the level a fairly long way above a gorge.

Before coming to a small chapel, open another iron gate. The little houses scattered about belong to the summer meadows of **Plátanos**. They are inhabited when there's work in the vineyards and fruit orchards.

Just before a broad scree slope you can see the highest point of the walk (775m). If you look to the left, you will see a broad mountain path going up

*Curious kids at the end of the walk.*

*View of the coastal village of Móhlos with the island of the same name.*

from the houses below and this is the path that you will ascend later. Turn left before the scree slope onto the path that leads to the houses. Once you have arrived at the vineyard adjoining them, go towards the right-hand house, open a gate in the wire fence to reach the mule path. It brings you along the right-hand edge of a gorge. The path again climbs to a height of 750m at a deserted settlement. The path swings to the left onto a roadway. After only a short time it goes through a wire gate and an enchanting panorama awaits you. The view reaches down to the sea and the villages of Sfáka, Tourlotí and Mirsíni. In 1992 the whole slope, from here down to the sea, was burnt in a fire.

On the first bend after the gate the old path curves round to the right. It cuts across the road now and again and considerably shortens the descent. However, be careful that you do not take paths branching off to terraces. When you come to a large reservoir made out of concrete, the walk's nearly over. Follow the road directly towards Tourlotí. Soon afterwards you go past a pump house from where the roadway leads onto the tarmac road. Walk along this into the village. The **Tourlotí** bus stop is right at the start of the village, by the bend in the road round the cemetery.

# 15 From Skopí to Faneroménis monastery

Faneroménis monastery

## Skopí – Moní Faneroménis – Sitía

**Starting point:** Skopí, on the road between Agios Nikólaos and Sitía, about 10km from Sitía.

**Walking times:** Skopí – road junction 1¼ hrs., descent to the sea 20 mins., first bay – monastery 25 mins., monastery – road junction 1 hr., road junction – Sitía 45 mins.; total time 3¾ hrs.

**Difference in height**: 250m descent on the way there, 100m ascent; 250m descent on the return, 150m ascent.

**Grade:** easy walk on tarmac and gravel, very hot in summer.

**Stops and accommodation:** numerous rooms and tavernas in Sitía.

**Bus connections:** several daily Agios Nikólaos – Sitía and in the opposite direction.

**Tip:** an ideal plan is to stop for a swim in the middle of this walk.

The winding road from Agios Nikólaos touches on a whole series of beautifully situated villages and continually surprises you with some wonderful views into the mountains as well as down to the coast.

The last big village before Sitía is **Skopí**. 500m after the end of the village, in the direction of Sitía, there's a newly concreted road leading up to the left (sign for 'Moní Faneroméni'). After about 1km the concrete stops and you walk along the gravel road past orchards and olive plantations (partly in the shade) to the north. The road runs along a chain of flat-topped hills so that you always have an open view down to the very green, deep valley. After more than an hour the road from Sitía joins from the right (signpost) and after a few minutes you will get your first clear view of the steep coast. The road zigzags for a good kilometre down the 150 vertical metres to the sea. The play of colours is fascinating, especially when the sun is low, with the almost white sandstone of the north coast contrasting with the deep blue sea and the luxuriant green of the valley. The road winds its way closely below the vertical rock faces near to the water in a westerly direction, crosses the first side valley and continues to lead close to the rocks into the second valley (taverna, open in the tourist season). In stormy seas this section of the path might be impassable. An ascent of 100 vertical metres follows, then you reach an extensive, flat-bottomed hollow, some newly built houses, small greenhouses and the large monastery of **Faneroménis** (Saint's name stemming from the Greek word 'to appear'). The monastery cells are in two blocks built in a semi-circle. The church literally clings to the edge of the land and gives you an open view into the deep canyon and out over the bay of Faneroménis.

For the return, take the 4km long gravel road at the road junction in the direction of Sitía, which crosses a flat hill, goes past isolated houses, greenhouses and orchards and leads leisurely downhill into the next valley. Just before the town boundary it reaches the main road (¾ hour walk from the junction). Since part of this route, especially on the inclines, is concreted, it is possible to do the whole of this route by car instead, although the section along beside the sea in particular might be in a very poor condition after rain and storms.

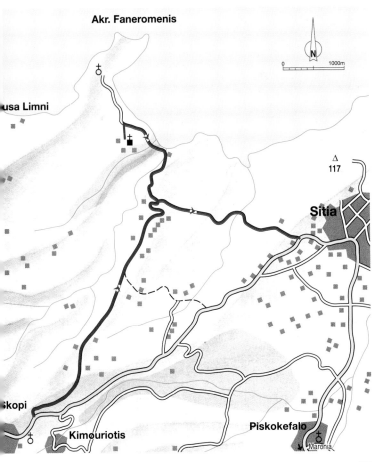

# 16 From Palékastro to Vái

From the table mountain to the palm beach

### Palékastro – Agáthia – port of Palékastro – sheep farm – Vái

**Starting point:** main square in Palékastro.
**Walking times:** Palékastro – Agáthia 10 mins., Agáthia – beach 15 mins., beach – harbour 25 mins., harbour – sheep farm just under 1¼ hrs., roadway 25 mins., roadway – path to Vái 30 mins.; total time 3 hrs.
**Difference in height:** 200m.
**Grade:** surefootedness and a lack of vertigo essential, also a sense of direction over sometimes rough ground. Good footwear, long trousers.
**Stops and accommodation:** tavernas and rooms in Palékastro.
**Bus connections:** several daily Sitía – Palékastro; Vái – Palékastro at 14.00.

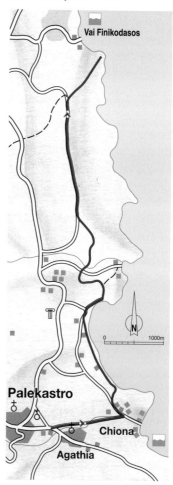

Start the walk in the main square in **Palékastro** and follow the road past the church in the direction of Agáthia. After 10 minutes you reach the entrance to the village of **Agáthia**. Take the turning off to Chiona Beach beforehand (sign), again heading straight for the table mountain. Carry straight on (do not turn off at the sign for Hotel Marina). At the foot of the table mountain follow the road to the left. There's a small track going to the beach on the left of the table mountain. Either walk along the beach or, more leisurely, just above on the track.
After walking for 50 minutes you come to the tarmac road at the end of the bay that comes from Palékastro to the little **fishing harbour**. Follow this to the right and walk past the harbour along the coastline.

56

*The sandy bay and Vái palm forest beyond.*

The path continues over the cliffs, high above the sea, until you can see a bay below after one hour. Keep along the ridge going inland in the direction of the wind farm in the distance and descend the crest. Shortly after a barbed wire fence crosses over a thick black pipe, a path leads down to the right. Follow a track below to the left until you come to a house with a castellated roof. On the opposite slope you can see a rocky outcrop, which comes down to the streambed. Walk as far as the start of the rocky outcrop and go along the inside of a fence until, after about 250m, you find your way through a gate. After a few metres you start the rough, sweat-making ascent up a scree gully (only for surefooted walkers who do not suffer from vertigo!). At the top of the ridge continue in a northerly direction and you soon come to a path that leads to a goat pen.

From here a broad, two-tracked roadway leads north. It runs almost on the level in the direction of a hill with a trig point. Just before it, after two hours walking, you pass a large gate. Ten minutes after that, the roadway goes round a big left-hand loop and a path branches off to the right. Take this path and go through a gully eastwards (now over rough terrain again) and keep heading towards the coast round a gentle left-hand bend until, over a mountain ridge, you come out directly at the rocks on the right above the palm beach at **Vái**.

# 17 Onto Pétsofas

Morning walk across quiet bays to the ancient summit shrine

## Agáthia – Pétsofas – Agáthia

**Starting point:** Agáthia, 1km from Palékastro.
**Walking times:** ascent 1 hr. descent 45 mins., total time 1¾ hrs.
**Difference in height:** 200m.
**Grade:** an easy walk with beautiful views down onto Chiona beach and the table

mountain. Do not forget to take sun protection with you.
**Bus connections:** six daily in the tourist season Sitía – Palékastro.
**Stops and accommodation:** tavernas, rooms and apartments in Palékastro, Agáthia and Chiona beach.

From the church in Agáthia turn right, past the Anatóli restaurant, then left onto the track leading out of the village. There's a yellow arrow on a brown background at a fork. Do not turn right shortly afterwards at a fork (Karoúmes Beach), follow the left-hand path instead (metal arrow). Then carry straight on through olive groves as far as a sign for the 'Peak Sanctuary'. Turn right here (arrow). Continue following the signs until, after a gate, a mountain path leads uphill to the summit shrine.
Return back along the same path.

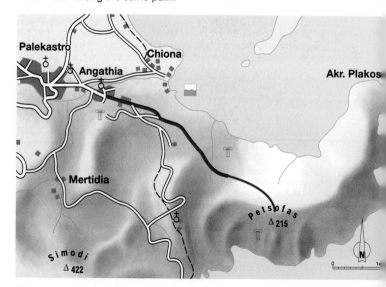

*View of Pétsofas from the table mountain.*

# 18 From Agáthia to Hohlakiés

Quiet gorges and bays on the east coast

## Agáthia – Skiniás bay – Karoúmes bay – Hohlakiés

**Starting point:** Agáthia, 1km from Palékastro.
**Walking times:** Agáthia – Skiniás bay 1½ hrs., Skiniás bay – Karoúmes bay 1 hr., Karoúmes bay – Hohlakiés a good 1¼ hrs.; total time just under 4 hrs.
**Difference in height:** ascent 250m, descent 150m.
**Grade:** varied scenery, easy. Sun protec-

tion, swimming gear, water and provisions.
**Bus connections:** six times daily in the tourist season Sitía – Palékastro – Vaí, twice daily Sitía – Palékastro – Hohlakiés – Zákros.
**Stops and accommodation:** tavernas in Palékastro and on the table mountain, rooms in Agáthia and Palékastro.

*Palékastro in front of the prominent table mountain at Chiona beach.*

Begin the walk at the church in **Agáthia**. At the next road go right and out of the village past the Anatoli restaurant. At the end of the tarmac there's a fork (wooden arrow with red and blue waymarkers). Following the waymarkers past a weekend house and fruit orchards, you come to another waymarker board (left turning here to the Petsofas shrine). Continue right to a cistern and beside a fence. Then take a path uphill right and towards a **little white church** that you reach through a gate. There are some derelict houses nearby.

Continue along a roadway in a southerly direction until you meet a roadway coming from Palékastro which is closed off by a fence. Climb over the fence and ascend the gentle slope up the roadway to a **col**. Then the roadway leads downhill between two gorges. At the last big bend in the road, a path branches off to the left, which, after 50m, is clearly marked in blue and brings you to the quiet **Skiniás bay** surrounded by rocky ledges. If you continue along the right-hand edge of the bay, you have to first go through a fence, before coming to the broad **Karoúmes bay**. From the beach take a path inland on the left-hand side of the streambed and take a shortcut over a rounded hill into the **Hohlakiés gorge** (or climb directly up the twisting streambed). The path keeps to the streambed (which might be impassable in winter or early spring due to the high level of the water), and in places you will need to use your hands to scramble over boulders.

The gorge opens out after an hour. Go through a gate and reach Hohlakiés 20 minutes later.

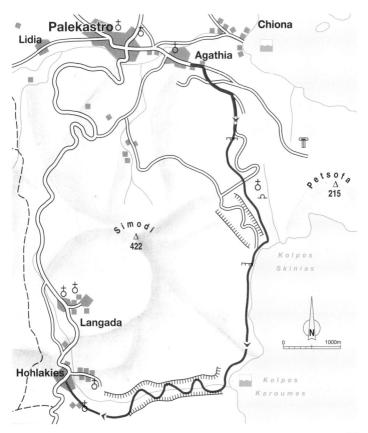

# 19 From Zákros to the Minoan palace of Káto Zákros

The valley of the dead – the 'Grand Canyon' of Crete

## Zákros – valley of the dead – Káto Zákros

**Starting point:** centre of Zákros.
**Walking times:** Zákros – gorge ½ hr., descent in the gorge 1½ hrs., gorge – palace – beach ¼ hr.; total time 2¼ hrs.
**Difference in height:** 350m.
**Grade:** easy gorge walk. Sun protection, swimming gear.
**Bus connections:** twice daily Sitía – Zákros.

**Stops and accommodation:** tavernas and rooms in Zákros and Káto Zákros.
**Alternative:** you can descend into the gorge after about 2.5km on the tarmac road from Zákros to Káto Zákros (sign says 'gorge'). It's one hour from here to the sea. Return from Káto Zákros to Zákros via the old road (beautiful views into the gorge).

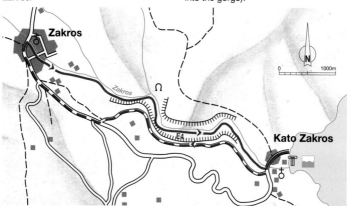

The path through the valley of the dead is one of the most beautiful walks in eastern Crete. The deeply cut gorge is closed off by vast, red rock faces and the Minoans used to bury their dead in its caves. Moreover, one of the four large Minoan palaces once stood between the entrance to the gorge and the sea.

Begin your walk in the centre of **Zákros** and turn left from the main square into the road, Odos *25 Martíou*. On the right before the church a path branches off leading downhill. Go under an aqueduct and along beside a water channel until you reach the south-eastern end of Zákros. After a quarter of an hour the concrete path becomes a gravel path. After 50m there's a fork where you carry straight on gently uphill.

*View down into the valley of the dead from the old road to Káto Zákros.*

Three minutes later you come to another fork. This time go left down a track, carry straight on and at a concreted bend in the roadway turn left down into the streambed. Continue following the waymarkings. The start of the gorge becomes more and more obvious. Past some plane trees and oleander bushes you come to a side valley joining from the left. At this point you cross over onto the right-hand side of the stream and continue along beside another water channel. After about 500m the path crosses the streambed again.

All at once you find yourselves amongst breathtaking scenery. Rock faces of up to 300m tower upwards all around you. The stream you have been following all of a sudden dries up (in winter you might possibly have to wade up to your knees through the water) and you're surrounded by a deathly silence. The reddish rocks are eroded and full of holes. The route through the streambed is an easy walk and eventually broadens out and leads through small banana plantations. You now meet the old roadway to Zákros, which crosses the streambed. Follow this to the left and you soon come past the excavation site of **Káto Zákros** palace. It's only another few minutes from here to the beautiful bay (tavernas).

**Return along the old road:** go back to the excavation site and cross the streambed on the gravel road that winds up to the upper edge of the gorge. The gravel becomes a tarmac road which takes you the 2.5km back to Zákros.

# 20 From Zákros to Zíros

Across the barren highlands of eastern Crete

### Zákros – Agios Geórgios chapel – Zíros

**Starting point:** Zákros.
**Walking times:** Zákros – 1st high valley 1 hr., 1st high valley – Agios Geórgios chapel ¾ hr., Agios Geórgios – 2nd high valley ½ hr., 2nd high valley – roadway ¾ hr., roadway – Zíros ½ hr.; total time 3½ hrs.
**Difference in height:** 200m.

**Grade:** easy walk, some route finding required. Good footwear, water, sun protection.
**Stops and accommodation:** tavernas and hotels in Zákros, two tavernas in Zíros.
**Bus connections:** at 7.30 and 14.30 Zíros – Sitía.

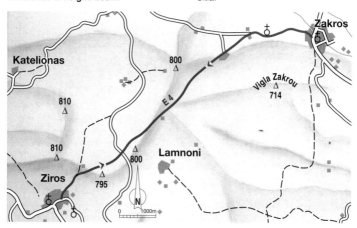

The walk begins in **Zákros**. Ascend the road, *Odos Elefterias*, through the village in a south-westerly direction up to the little church of **Apano Iglesia**. From here there are good E4 waymarkers to Ziros. A vigorous spring emerges below the church which supplies the village with water and continues to flow through the valley of the dead. The spring is surrounded by shady plane trees.

Go 30m to the left from the little church, then through a gate. The once broad, paved path starts here. During the ascent you are rewarded with a beautiful view of the little white square houses of the village of Zákros. Your gaze sweeps across the valley of the dead down to the sea. The greenhouses, where they grow primarily bananas in this area, shine in the sunlight. After about an hour of steady climbing you reach a hollow at the top.

Go straight across this through gates on a broad path. About 80m further on continue along the broad path, but then don't take the roadway uphill, go left instead along the old, stony mule path into a cleft (water pipe). You should wear sturdy shoes for this section of the path. After half an hour to three quarters you arrive unexpectedly at the **chapel of Agios Geórgios** near the deserted village of Skália (the short ascent to Skália is worth the effort with its view of the eastern coastline from above the ruins). The chapel beside the path has a covered veranda, so that you could contemplate sheltering there or making an overnight stop. There's a spring just above it, but this is possibly dry in summer.

The mule path continues uphill past the chapel, some vineyards and derelict houses and in the same direction through a countryside strewn with weather-beaten rock. Then it goes along the stony path over barren hills until you come to another high valley with vineyards and some little houses. Go round this second high valley on an easy left-hand bend, then a tedious path starts through the stony wasteland. Keep heading towards a distant radio mast, then the path crosses over a roadway which leads to the mast. You can already see the valley of Ziros below. Another good half an hour brings you downhill, then the path ends at the upper houses of Ziros at a water container. The church of Agía Paraskeví is worth taking a look at. It was built in 1523 and is painted with frescoes.

**Path from Zíros to Zákros:** from the square in Ziros head past some houses towards a cleft going up to the east and following the E4 waymarkers ascend the cleft. After 25 minutes go through a gate, and 10 minutes later you cross a roadway going through another gate immediately afterwards. Continue in the same direction along the stony path over the chain of hills covered in low, prickly *phrygana* (scrub), always in a north-easterly direction. After 50 minutes go through another gate. After another 35 minutes you reach a small high valley covered with vines and you go round the left side of this past derelict houses. You will soon see the dilapidated houses of Skália with **Agios Geórgios chapel** below. Behind the church the once paved mule path continues left downhill and exactly one hour after the small high valley, comes to another one. It was once similarly planted with vines, but has now been ploughed up into farmland. A broad path leads across which is closed off at the beginning and at the end with a gate. Immediately after the last gate follow the *yellow arrow* uphill to the left and the old paved path descends shortly afterwards to **Zákros**.

# 21 From Maroniá to Praisós

To the acropolis of Praisós

**Maroniá – Praisós – Maroniá**

**Starting point:** Maroniá, 12km south of Sitía, situated on the main highway to Ierápetra.

**Walking times:** Maroniá – cemetery 15 mins., cemetery – junction 25 mins., junction – Praisós 50 mins., return a good 1¼ hrs.; total time 3 hrs.

**Difference in height:** ascent 300m, descent 300m.

**Grade:** easy walk, but a good sense of direction necessary, at times along gravel roads. Shade in places, very hot in summer.

**Stops and accommodation:** tavernas and *kafeníon* in Maroniá, rooms in Sitía.

**Bus connections:** several daily Sitía – Ierápetra.

From the road at the upper edge of **Maroniá**, descend into the lower part of the village down to the church (you can park in front of the church). There's a good view from there of the whole route of the path – up the valley to the cemetery, into the left side valley and up the hill on the right, recognizable by the many olive plantations, as far as the solitary tall trees at the top. The ancient site of Praisós lies on this rounded hill.

The church lies directly by the drop into the river valley and from here there's a narrow concrete road leading downhill to the right into the valley. Just before the road meets another one in the valley bottom, a path on the right, lined with cypress trees, goes up to the cemetery (beautiful view back to Maroniá). From the cemetery go down a steep path to the road which runs near to the stream. Follow this up the stream, crossing over the stream several times. The gravel road leads into the left valley with two thick water pipes along the side. Ignore the next gravel road leading steeply up to the right. Then the stream forces its way through a narrow place in the rocks ahead and after crossing the stream twice it continues up the right-hand bank. 100m after the narrow section (large old concrete slabs on the left by the water) a track leads steeply up to the right past a stone hut and runs up

*Remains of the acropolis at Praisós.*

across the slope planted with olive trees. You come to a broader gravel road that you ascend to the right. For the return route: look out for an old derelict house on the right between the olive trees when finding your way on the return. As you look back there are many views of the valley and the village of Maroniá beyond. On the next left-hand bend go straight up the steep path (shorter) or continue left round the bend. At the following fork the path continues round an S-bend uphill. (A tip for the descent later: keep descending the steep slope on the dirt road, ignore turnings off right until you come to the previously mentioned S-bend).

After a 50-minute steep ascent you have reached the ancient site of **Praisós**. The remains of solitary pillars, quarried slabs and stones and water troughs are the visible signs of the post Minoan town founded by the Eteocretans, dating from the 12th century BC and stretching out over three hills. Through the rusty gate (a board says 'First Acropolis') there's a short detour up onto the hill on the small plain. Here are to be found the remains of the acropolis. The tiny village of Nea Praisós lies above about 2km away.

Return the same way. If you should get lost on the descent and end up higher in the valley, you can follow the watercourse without any great problem downstream until you meet the road again near the start of the walk.

# Lassíthi plateau and Díkti mountains

The predominant characteristics of Crete's landscape are the many plateaus and the high, inaccessible mountain ranges. The Lassíthi plateau, the most beautiful and impressive plateau, is situated in the east of the island. It lies at an altitude of 850m, is almost circular, has an area of 48 sq.km. and is surrounded by high mountains. It has been inhabited from the earliest times and because of its temperate climate has always been used intensively for agriculture. During the time of the Venetian occupation large quantities of corn were exported to Italy. Several trading routes, still intact in some places, date from this period and they lead from the plain down into the surrounding villages. But the historiography goes back much further. One of the most important cult sites of Greek mythology, the Diktaíon cave, where according to legend, Zeus came into the world, lies here above the village of Psihró and is a must on the tourist itinerary for most visitors to Crete.

Up until a few years ago the landscape of the Lassíthi plateau was characterized by hundreds of windmills covered with white sails, but unfortunately this scene is now a thing of the past since all except a few of them have been replaced with diesel pumps.

There's a series of beautiful hikes and mountain ascents to be made in this region. The climate is temperate due to the altitude so that almost ideal conditions prevail throughout the year. The exception, of course, is the high Díkti massif which are covered extensively in snow until late spring.

There are also some rewarding hiking routes which come down from the plain to Krássi and Vrahási or to Kritsá, one of the most beautiful villages on Crete – all of them impressive walks through an exceptional landscape. The

*Once covered with thousands of windmills, the Lassíthi plateau today.*

*Prominent holm oak in the Díkti mountains.*

same goes for the ascent of Kastamonítsa along the western edge of the plain. The nearer you come to the southern edge of the Lassíthi plateau, the more remote and less developed the area. The somewhat easier and shorter mountain walk onto Aféndis or the isolated ascent path over Cámpos Máni to Xeniákos are a foretaste of the most dramatic and inaccessible mountain massif on Crete, the Díkti mountains.

The third largest massif on Crete with the three main peaks of Lázaros, Díkti and Aféndis Hristós has for a long time been forgotten and it is not easily reached. The almost alpine ascent routes are serious mountain excursions that require stamina, the relevant mountain experience and appropriate equipment. In return, they can be rewarding hikes which take you into especially impressive landscapes. The European E4 long distance path running from west to east on the island (white sign with black and yellow) also goes through this remote mountain region. It follows an ancient shepherds' path directly through the massif to the east down to Selákano, a secluded high valley to the east of the Díkti mountains which is rich in water. This is the start of the most forested region on Crete. Extensive fir and pine forests cover the foothills a long way to the east and south, as far down as the coastal regions of Ierápetra. The big forest fires of recent years, often caused by carelessness, have inflicted unimaginable damage here.

# 22 From Kastamonítsa to Káto Metóhi

Historic gateways to the Lassíthi plateau

## Kastamonítsa – Tíhos – Káto Metóhi

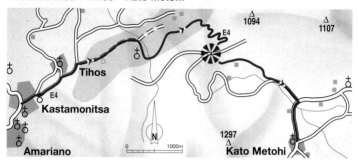

**Starting point:** Kastamonítsa, 550m, situated 7km east of Kastélli.

**Walking times:** Kastamonítsa – start of the mule path 45 mins., mule path – start of the Venetian road 45 mins., Venetian road – col 1 hr., col – Lassíthi plateau 45 mins.; total time 3½ hrs.

**Difference in height:** ascent 600m, descent 150m.

**Grade:** easy walk, good route finding (E4 waymarkers).

Possible all year round, very hot in summer, partly shady on the ascent.

**Stops and accommodation:** rooms and tavernas in Kastélli as well as in the villages on the Lassíthi plateau.

**Bus connections:** several daily Iráklion – Kastélli, only one a day as far as Kastamonítsa, from the village of Psihró (Diktaíon cave) several buses daily to Iráklion and Agios Nikólaos.

**Tip:** the site of ancient Lythós at Xídas (town dating back to the Hellenistic period).

The narrow road to Tíhos branches off to the north in **Kastamonítsa**. Follow this past the last houses as far as an high old wall with a church. Afterwards there's a fork. Left goes down into the nearby village of Tíhos, but you go right along the broad gravel road that runs almost on the level, but later gently downhill, across the hillside (*E4 waymarkers from here onwards*). At the next fork you follow the lower road and after about 2km come past a beautifully enclosed spring. 1km further on, before a small gorge, you reach the small chapel of **Agios Geórgios**. After crossing the gorge an old mule path turns off right uphill (E4), ascends the very overgrown slope and offers some shade in places. Sometimes it goes over well-preserved paving stones and old water channels can still be seen at the edge of the path. After ascending for half an hour you come to the almost 3m wide Venetian trading path which you follow uphill.

*Old Venetian trading path onto the Lassíthi plateau.*

This section of old road construction, on which the mule and donkey cara-vans used to transport the produce from the Lassíthi plateau down to the vil-lages and towns, zigzags up the hillside and reaches a col at a height of 950m. The building of new roads has destroyed the last hundred metres to the top of the pass.

There's a good view on both sides, of the villages in the west and of the nearby, almost circular plateau in the east. Carry straight on along the gravel road which leads to the Lassíthi plateau. After 100m you can see the old path on the left below. However, not until after 200m (*E4 signpost*), do you climb left along a narrow path onto a small, flat col area and from there down a section without a path to the again well-preserved, old mule path (the E4 continues along the considerably longer gravel road to the gate). It leads down the valley and ends at a gate. It continues on the other side as a gravel road. After only 15 minutes you come to the road at the edge of the Lassíthi plateau, just before the village of **Káto Metóhi**.

# 23 From Tzermiádo to Krássi

From the Lassíthi plateau to the biggest plane tree on Crete

### Tzermiádo – Níssimos plain – Krássi

**Starting point:** health centre (Kentro Ygias) in Tzermiádo; compare with Walk 24.

**Walking times:** health centre in Tzermiádo – Níssimos plain 30 mins., crossing the plain 15 mins., end of the plain – mountain ridge 20 mins., mountain ridge – roadway 30 mins., roadway – Krássi 30 mins.; total time 2 hrs.

**Difference in height:** ascent 150m, de-scent 400m.

**Grade:** good footwear, surefootedness and route finding required.

**Stops and accommodation:** tavernas and rooms in Tzermiádo; tavernas in Krássi.

**Bus connections:** Iráklion – Tzermiádo at 8.30 and 14.30; Agios Nikólaos – Tzermiádo at 8.30 and 14.00 ; Lassíthi pla-teau – Krássi – Iráklion at 14.00 and 17.00.

It's best to travel to the starting point of this walk on the Lassíthi plateau by bus which leaves Iráklion at 8.30 (9.00 at the turn-off to Kastélli in Hersónissos). Ask the driver to drop you off at the health centre in Tzermiádo (Kentro Ygias).

From the health centre follow the main road in the direction of **Tzermiádo,**

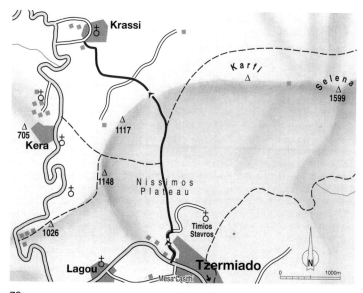

*Blossoming wild flowers along the path to Krássi in the spring.*

as far as a sign 'To the Timios Stavros Church' after a few hundred metres which indicates to the left. A gravel path leads gently uphill onto the **Níssimos plain**.

Go straight across the plain along the main reddish dirt path towards the lowest point of the surrounding mountains in the north. The path leads you naturally back into the stony landscape. Leave the plain at an iron gate (re-used bedstead). The path between the rocks is not waymarked, but is easy to follow due to the red tracks on the pale stones. After 15 minutes going uphill (just under 1 hr. from the health centre) you are almost at the top where the path forks. Take the left-hand branch up to the mountain ridge and climb left into a hollow that you walk through to the other end. Then follows a short section of climbing (II+) and the crossing of a cirque. The path now heads towards a dirt road, which is already visible. Cross the slope through a holm oak wood. Cross over an area of scree and eventually descend to a sheep trough and to the start of the dirt road (30 mins. descent from the pass). After a quarter of an hour along the roadway you reach a terraced slope in front of which the path makes an obvious bend to the right. Twenty minutes further down, the path divides and you continue through olive trees to the right. Before a rocky projection a path joins from the left, which you ignore. Follow the black water pipes and after about an hour's descent arrive in **Krássi**, where you will find the square on the right with the water house and the largest plane tree on Crete whose trunk has a circumference of almost 16 metres.

# 24 From Tzermiádo to Vrahási

From the Lassíthi plateau to the national highway between Iráklion – Agios Nikólaos

### Tzermiádo – Níssimos plain – Agios Geórgios – Vrahási

**Starting point:** health centre (Kentro Ygias) in Tzermiádo (Lassíthi plateau).

**Walking times:** health centre in Tzermiádo – Níssimos plain 30 mins., crossing the plain 15 mins., end of the plain – mountain ridge 20 mins., round the mountain and descent without paths to the roadway 25 mins., roadway – sheep farm 1½ hrs., sheep farm – Agios Geórgios 35 mins., Agios Geórgios – bus stop in Vrahási 45 mins.; total time 4 hrs.

**Difference in height:** ascent 200m, descent 850m.

**Grade:** stamina and a good sense of direction required, adequate footwear, provisions and sun protection.

**Stops and accommodation:** restaurants and hotels in Tzermiádo.

**Bus connections:** Iráklion – Tzermiádo at 8.30 and 14.30; Agios Nikólaos – Tzermiádo at 8.30 and 14.00. From Vrahási in the direction of Iráklion or Agios Nikólaos.

The ideal time for this long and demanding walk is at the end of April, beginning of May, when the apple and quince trees are in blossom on the Lassíthi plateau and only a thin covering of snow remains on the slope of the Díkti mountains.

*Animal pens beside the path in Tzermiádo.*

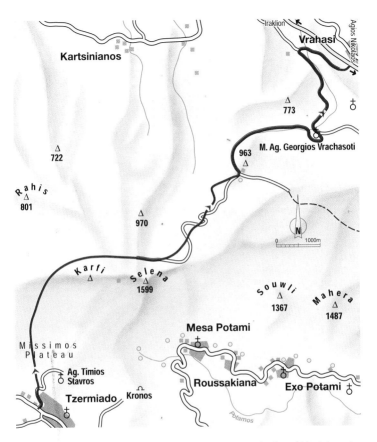

It's best to travel to the starting point of this walk on the Lassíthi plateau by bus, which leaves Iráklion at 8.30 (9.00 at the turn-off to Kastélli in Hersónissos). Ask the driver to drop you off at the bus stop at the health centre in Tzermiádo (Kentro Ygias), just before the first houses of the village. You will therefore need to start the walk at about 10.30.

From the health centre follow the main road in the direction of **Tzermiádo**, as far as a sign 'To the Timios Stavros Church' after a few hundred metres which indicates to the left. A gravel path leads gently uphill and allows you a beautiful view of the Lassíthi plateau if you look back. After about half an

*Whole hillsides are covered with yellow flowering gorse.*

hour you are almost submerged in a sea of stones. The **Níssimos plain** is reached shortly afterwards.

Do not continue in the direction of Timios Stavros, but go instead straight across the plain along the red earthen main path towards the lowest point of the surrounding mountains in the north. Leave the plain at an iron gate (re-used bedstead). The path between the rocks is not waymarked but is easy to follow due to the red tracks on the pale stones. After ascending for 15 minutes you are almost at the top there's an obvious fork. Take the right fork here. Some of the cairns are not that easy to see. After about an hour's walking towards the mountain ridge you eventually reach the top. If you are lucky, you will arrive directly by a small rusty metal sign.

Now begins a section without paths. Climb over the ridge and gently down into a hollow and towards a second ridge. The route is over rough ground, at first almost on the level around the mountain of Selena. After 20 minutes you will discover the path again and on a slight incline, come down to the upper end of a high-rising valley. After a good 1¾ hours, at a shady oak tree, the path meets a roadway coming up from below and you turn right onto this.

25 minutes later you reach some fencing and the roadway now leads downhill round a few bends. (If you want to take a shortcut, take the narrow path right after the fencing and walk along this for five minutes. Ignore the roadway branching off to the left shortly afterwards). You can see the sea through a broad cleft in the valley on the left and the flat countryside in front. After an hour walking along the roadway another roadway joins from above right, which you ignore, and half an hour later the roadway goes round a wide loop to the left at a sheep farm and a rainwater collector. Take a shortcut across the bend by following a narrow path, just before the sharp left-hand bend, that leads past the **sheep farm** and the rainwater collector and meets the roadway again further down. In another 35 minutes you arrive at the church of **Agios Geórgios**. The houses of Vrahási are already visible spreading across the hillside.

Continue along the roadway until you go past the church on its left hand side (exactly 4 minutes!). Then you descend a small path on the right between olive trees and bushes (6 minutes) until soon afterwards a track continues to the left. After five minutes a path branches off right across the riverbed. However, stay on this side and go for a short way along the roadway slightly uphill to the left. There's an amazing abundance of flowers in this valley: sage, oregano, thyme, sea squills, lilies, cistus in all colours, overlaid with the sweet scent of the yellow gorse.

Now cross over the streambed (25 minutes after Agios Geórgios). The roadway continues on the other side in the same direction and another path joins from the right after four minutes. One minute later you come to a road junction. Carry on straight ahead. The path soon runs down into the valley bottom and is paved in places, then abruptly goes up to the road. Gently ascend this road for another quarter of an hour until you reach the **Vrahási** bus stop on the national highway (be careful of the busy traffic!).

# 25 From Kritsá to the Lassíthi plateau

In the shadow of Díkti and Lázaros

### Kritsá – Katharó plateau – Lassíthi plateau

**Starting point:** Kritsá, 11km from Agios Nikólaos.
**Walking times:** Kritsá – Katharó plateau 4½ hrs., crossing the Katharó plateau 1¾ hrs., descent to the Lassíthi plateau 1 hr.; total time 7¼ hrs.
**Difference in height:** ascent 985m, descent 495m.
**Grade:** good fitness and a sense of direc-

tion required.
Sturdy footwear, sun protection, water and provisions.
**Bus connections:** frequent bus service between Agios Nikólaos and Kritsá; twice daily between Agios Nikólaos and Lassíthi plateau.
**Stops and accommodation:** tavernas and rooms in Kritsá and Tzermiádo.

Agios Nikólaos and its surrounding area are a good starting point for many walks. The village of Kritsá is just a stone's throw away, from whose terraces the visitor can gaze upon a sea of countless almond and olive trees. If you go up from Kritsá through the rock-strewn landscape, you will come to the Katharó plateau situated at 1130m, which is surrounded by the over 2000m high peaks of the Díkti mountains. The climate is considerably harsher than on the Lassíthi plateau (850m), your destination for this walk.

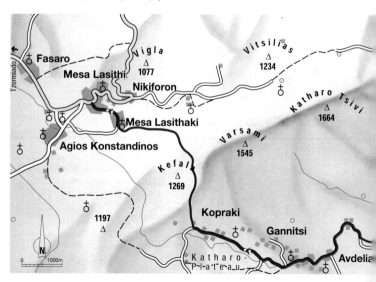

Start the walk by going up along the main road in **Kritsá** until you come to a sign 'Plateau of Katharó'. Before the sign turn into *Kritsapoúla street* and after 30m take the steps left up the tiny street of *Alexojanni* to the north-western end of the village. At this point you come back to the road to Katharó and the footpath begins opposite (*red and blue arrow*).

After 20 minutes you reach the road again. Follow this for five minutes then leave it to the right before a bridge and go uphill beside some terraces. After an hour you again meet the road onto which you turn left. After five minutes a path turns off left again which crosses the road once more 30 minutes later. From now on the route finding becomes a bit difficult since the scant waymarkers are not easy to find in this strange landscape of holm oak bushes and rock formations and it's easier to walk along the road, but you should at least be able to take a shortcut across the last big road bend. Then it's not much further to the **top of a pass** (a total of 4 hrs. up to here), from which you will descend in half an hour (100 vertical metres) onto the **Katharó plateau**.

The walk along the edge of the plain lasts about an hour. Follow the road into the village of **Giannítsi** and keep right at the fork in the road there. Ten minutes later a path branches off right (waymarker), which then goes past a gorge on the right. The well-marked path leads through a sea of rocks and then gradually ascends over terraced land until the view opens out onto the

Lassíthi plateau below. Continue following the waymarkers to the right and eventually you descend on the right-hand side through a cleft into the valley. You walk across terraces to reach the **Lassíthi plateau**.

It's a quarter of an hour to the first village of **Mésa Lassitáki** and another quarter of an hour to **Mésa Lassíthi**. You can find a place to stay overnight in either **Tzermiádo** (the Kronion restaurant can be recommended) or **Agios Geórgios**, which are 4km away from each other.

# 26 From the Lassíthi plateau to Kritsá

From windmills to almond trees

## Mésa Lassíthi – Tápes – Kritsá

**Starting point:** Mésa Lassíthi on the Lassíthi plateau.
**Walking times:** Mésa Lassíthi – 1st chapel 1 hr., 1st chapel – 2nd chapel ¾ hr., 2nd chapel – water-house 1 hr., water-house – Tápes 1½ hrs., Tápes – Kritsá 1¾ hrs.; total time 6¼ hrs.
**Difference in height:** ascent 330m, descent 830m.

**Grade:** a walk requiring good fitness and a sense of direction.
Good footwear, sun protection, water and provisions.
**Bus connections:** Agios Nikólaos – Lassíthi plateau twice a day; Kritsá – Agios Nikólaos frequent bus service.
**Stops and accommodation:** tavernas and rooms in Tzermiádo and Kritsá.

**Mésa Lassíthi**, the starting point of your walk, lies at the eastern edge of the Lassíthi plateau. The road to Agios Nikólaos leaves the plateau here and this is the point where you start the walk. Not long afterwards you walk through the area of **Nikifóron**. 20 minutes after the start of the walk turn right on a sharp hairpin bend and take the mule path uphill (not the gravel path downhill). Follow this for about 15 minutes and you will meet a gravel road (right). This runs in a long left-hand loop uphill and on the left-hand side you

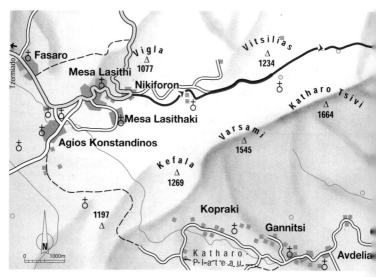

can look down over the Potámi valley. After 50 minutes you come to a **stone chapel**.

At the back of the church (apse) continue along the path and take the gravel road joining from the right after 12 minutes. After seven minutes go left at the fork. At the next fork (one minute later) turn up right through a fence. If you look down to the left, you will see shepherds' huts above a valley cleft. Stay on the gravel road until you come to a grey chapel after 1½ hours. 300m further on you pass a trough with spring water. Go past this to the left and soon ascend the gravel road up a moderate incline. After two hours the gravel road comes to an end and becomes a small path. After crossing some scree you reach a **water-house**, and after that cross over a gully (be careful if it's wet!). Ten minutes later the view opens out over the Mirabello gulf and the town of Agios Nikólaos. Below Vitsílias (1234m) the path heads directly towards Nikólaos. The church tower of Tápes appears a little later. Go through a fence and continue downhill along the left edge of the valley, then along beside a fence until the start of a track. Follow this to **Tápes.**

Carry on along the road past the church through the village. At the end of the second part of the village there's a *kafeníon*, where you can also order a simple meal. Continue past the *kafeníon* down between two houses until you come to a fork. Go downhill right to a streambed across which you come to a roadway on the right that immediately becomes a path again and

goes up an incline. There's a gate in a fence just afterwards.

The path now stays above the cleft of the valley. Half an hour from the *kafeníon* you go through another gate and shortly after that past a building.

A roadway starts here which brings you to the broad road leading from Kritsá to Lató. Turn right to complete the last part of the walk to Kritsá.

But if you haven't been to **Lató** yet, don't miss an opportunity to visit it and turn left here instead.

# 27 Across the Lassíthi plateau

From the cave of Zeus in Psihró to Tzermiádo

## Psihró – Lassíthi plateau – Tzermiádo

**Starting point:** car park below Psihró cave (Dikteon Andron).
**Walking time:** 1¼ hrs.
**Difference in height:** none.
**Grade:** quite an easy walk on roads through fields.

**Stops and accommodation:** tavernas and rooms in Psihró, Tzermiádo and other villages on the Lassíthi plateau.
**Bus connections:** twice daily from Iráklion and Agios Nikólaos to the Lassíthi plateau.

Your walk begins at the large **car park** below the cave of Zeus. If you look across the Lassíthi plateau from here, you can see on the right of the car park a paved path leading down into the village of **Psihró**. At the western end of the village there are some signposts pointing in all directions. Cross over the road and go straight onto an asphalt path into the fields past fruit trees. If you do this walk in late autumn you will see bright yellow fields that have been harvested. Donkeys graze on the dry grass which has been left and you will occasionally see farmers picking potatoes. The fertile plain is planted with potatoes, corn, fruit and vegetables.

The path runs parallel to the road leading past the village of Psihró. After five minutes there's a fork where you take the path bending round to the right. Carry straight on six minutes later at a crossroads. There's a small hill ahead of you in the distance. At the next fork seven minutes later carry straight on along a path with windmills. The much talked-about windmills are a sad and depressing sight today, as many of them are only rusty wrecks. The pictures with thousands of white linen sails blowing in the wind are a thing of the past. It is diesel pumps that have been bringing the water to the surface for irrigation purposes for a long time now. Keep left at the next turn-off two minutes later. Go down another road with windmills, this time in a northerly direction. Three minutes later, at a little concrete bridge, walk along beside a ditch again in an easterly direction towards the hill which you were heading for earlier. Carry straight on at the next crossroads beside the ditch. If you want to get an idea of where Tzermiádo is situated, keep a look-out after a large, white building that is the high school of Tzermiádo at the north-eastern edge of the Lassíthi plateau.

Go left again at the next crossroads, to the north. For 20 minutes follow the good path in a northerly direction. Go straight on at the next crossroads. Fifty minutes later a path leads off left to a little church in a fenced-off square in the middle of some shady trees, but you go straight ahead. The little church marks the middle point of the Lassíthi plateau. There are no more turnings off this path for a long while now. At the next obvious crossroads turn to the right and keep directly towards the village of Tzermiádo still a way

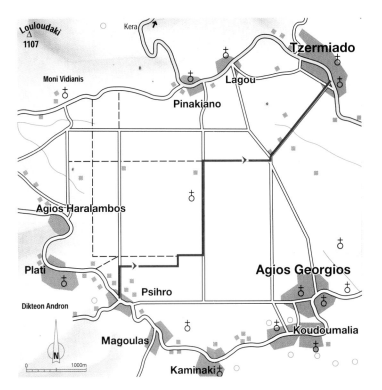

off in the distance. Five minutes later at a three-way junction carry straight on until you cross a streambed over a bridge. At the following crossroads go immediately right and along the left-hand side of the ditch. The road runs beside apple and walnut trees directly into Tzermiádo.

A few hundred metres before the village there's another crossroads which is no longer confusing since you can clearly see your destination ahead. After 1¼ hours you have reached **Tzermiádo**. Go right at a stop sign and then immediately left past the OTE (telegraph office). You arrive in the centre of the village directly by the Kronion restaurant which is highly recommended.

# 28 Onto Aféndis, 1578m

Round walk through the western Díkti mountains

## Moní Vidianís – Aféndis – Platí

**Starting point:** Vidianís monastery at the western edge of the Lassíthi plateau, on the road Káto Metóhi – Pinakianó.
**Walking times:** road – top of the ridge 1 hr., top of the ridge – start of the footpath 45 mins., start of the footpath – stone hut 45 mins., stone hut – summit 1 hr., summit – col 30 mins., col – Platí 1½ hrs.; total time 5½-6 hrs.
**Difference in height:** ascent 800m, descent 800m.
**Grade:** moderately difficult mountain walk

with fabulous views, hard-going over some sections of rough terrain (about a third of the walk), route finding needed, no shade, no drinking water along the whole way.
**Stops and accommodation:** good choice of rooms and tavernas on the west side of the Lassíthi plateau in the villages of Agios Haralambós, Platí, Psihró, Magoulás.
**Bus connections:** twice daily to Psihró, once daily to Káto Metóhi.

The western Díkti mountains tower over the Lassíthi plateau at 800m. Aféndis, 1578m, is a mountain that gives the most spectacular views from its summit chapel. The quickest ascent is from Platí, but much more pleasant is the route described here.

*Summit chapel on Aféndi, 1578m.*

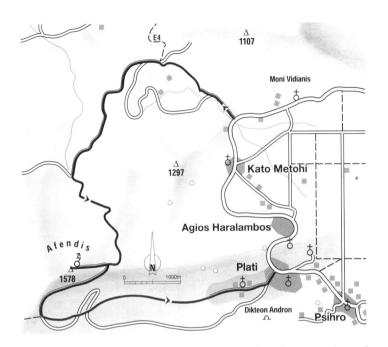

A side valley runs up to the north-west just before the **monastery of Vidianís** and this is where the walk begins. Follow the gravel road for about 1km up the valley to a left-hand bend. Leave the road here by going straight on and continue along the dirt road, then a paved mule path which brings you after 30 minutes onto a 950m **high pass**. As the road running above has buried the last part of the path, you have to climb up left to the road. You reach the top of the pass and a road junction after 200m. The old mule path descends on the west side straight down to Tíhos (*E4 waymarkers*), while you follow the roadway left (in a south-westerly direction).

The road zigzags up round wide bends across the bare mountain slopes where there are only a few solitary trees, otherwise low prickly bushes. The view gets better and better down to the Lassíthi plateau and over to the north coast, past the island of Día to Iráklion. The Psilorítis massif rises in the west. The road runs gently uphill for about 2km on the west side of the mountain, then leads left round a loop into a small side valley. Exactly on the bend (at a height of 1050m), at a solitary tree, you leave the road and follow a narrow path ascending southwards in the valley cleft. The path ascends across small plains, rugged ledges and eroded holes, as well as frequent hollows and flat basins. Past two fenced-off iron containers there follows a short descent across ledges into a lower depression. Here and there you will see some large shady oak trees, which are inviting places to stop for a rest. The path now heads towards the hillside opposite. You can see a **stone hut** at the top between two trees, your next destination, with the mountains of Díkti and Aféndis Hristós in the background that are still heavily covered in snow in the spring. After a steep ascent without paths you come directly past a deep, open cistern and 100m after that reach the **hut** (1350m). There's another beautiful view down to the Lassíthi plateau. After the hut ascend the increasingly steeper slope without paths in a south-westerly direction, mostly over scree and firm rock until you reach a flat ridge which runs further up westwards to the summit.

After 40 minutes you come to the summit of **Aféndis** (1578m) at the left edge of the ridge (in high winds you should keep in the wind-protected hollows). The simple dome is built out of uncut limestone and the summit chapel is dedicated to the Holy Trinity. A new radio tower has been erected next

*View eastwards across the fertile Lassíthi plateau.*

*View from the summit of Aféndis of Díkti (left) and Aféndis Hristós (right).*

to it. From here at the top there's a magnificent panorama over the eastern part of Crete up to the circle of mountain ranges: villages, roads, vineyards, mountains – amongst others Kófinas, Joúhtas, Psilorítis, Kouloúkonas, the Sélena mountains and closeby, Aféndis Hristós and Díkti. In the north you can see the sea.

For the descent to Platí it's best to take the new gravel road as far as the flat col south-west of Aféndis. Now descend to the east. On the left-hand side of the valley a mostly distinct path runs downhill and crosses the road twice. The path eventually becomes a dirt road and goes past agricultural build-ings towards the nearby village. The last part is then concreted. A road from the left, coming from the church, brings you in a few minutes to **Platí** at the edge of the Lassíthi plateau.

If you do the walk in the opposite direction, turn off uphill on the main road directly by the *kafeníon* at a large electricity pylon.

# 29 From Magoulás through the mountains to Xeniákos

Along old transport paths through the western Díkti mountains

## Magoulás – Campus Máni – Xeniákos / Embaros

**Starting point:** Magoulás at the south-western edge of the Lassíthi plateau.
**Walking times:** Magoulás – col (1250m) 1½ hrs., col – Campus Máni 1 hr., Campus Máni – col 40 mins., col – 2nd hollow – col 40 mins., col – Xeniákos 1¼ hrs.; total time 5-5½ hrs.
**Difference in height:** ascent 650m, descent 850m.
**Grade:** long, moderately difficult walk along partly narrow, rocky and indistinct

paths through beautiful mountain valleys. Hardly any shade and no water along the way. Best time in spring and autumn. Good footwear necessary.
**Stops and accommodation:** places to stay overnight and tavernas in Magoulás and in the other villages on the Lassíthi plateau. Simple rooms, tavernas and *kafeníon* in Embaros.
**Bus connections:** from Embaros there's a bus service to Iráklion and Ierápetra.

*Campus Máni, a remote high valley in the Díkti mountains.*

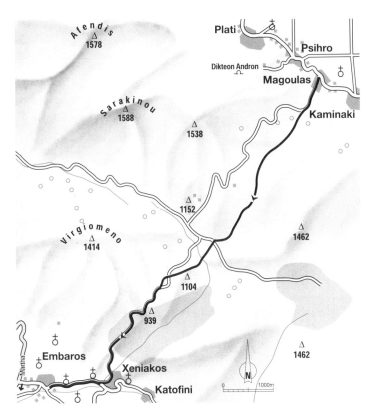

At the eastern end of Magoulás, opposite the Diónissos taverna (overnight stops), a road leads to the upper houses. Go southwards past these, on the right-hand side of the valley, towards the mountains. The road goes up the valley past orchards and sheep farms and you will see the milk urns standing ready in the morning on the road. After about 2km follow the roadway at a junction downhill to the left which ends after another kilometre at the last sheep farm in the valley bottom. About 150m before the sheep farm the old path goes up to the right. To start with it keeps almost on the level across old terraces towards the end of the valley, then leads across the left-hand side of the valley up to the top. Just before you reach the top of the ridge the path becomes quite indistinct and you now orientate yourself by the flat hollow on the left-hand side of the col. After a 1½ hour ascent you reach the col. It then goes past two large solitary trees into the next hollow.

the now obvious path descends in a south-westerly direction across terraces at the right-hand edge into the increasingly narrower valley. On the left you can just see the summit of Aféndis Hristós. The old mule path that is still well preserved in places, then leads for a long stretch above terraces along the edge of the valley. A gravel road joins from the left out of a small side valley and 20 minutes along this brings you to a wide valley bottom (at 1000m), the **Cámpos Máni**. Large stately oak trees stand in front of the green mountain slopes and the Díkti mountains rise up in the background, still often covered with snow in early summer.

From the stone hut go about 100m in a westerly direction, then left up the slope by four large oak trees. The road leads over a col down into another small valley. You can take a shortcut from the last long left-hand bend along an old paved section of path which leads steeply downhill on the right. At a solitary oak tree the paved mule path reaches the road again which goes along the right-hand edge of the small basin-shaped valley up to the top of the next col. At the top of the flat-topped hill leave the road to the left, go directly past the small trees into the start of a valley where there's another narrow footpath.

It leads down into the steeper and increasingly narrow valley. The slopes are again densely overgrown with prickly bushes. You can already see the first villages on the plain ahead. Now follows a short, steep descent through

*The donkey is rarely used for transport or riding today.*

*A chapel in the Díkti mountains, freshly white-washed for Easter.*

loose scree, then you reach the road again running below, directly at a **cave**. Continue down this on the right in the direction of Xeniákos (on the left of the road sheep enclosures with several feeding troughs). The gravel track continues further downhill through extensive olive plantations and after several bends reaches the road linking Xeniákos – Embaros. The bus station can be found in Embaros, 1½ km away.

# 30 From Embaros to Ano Viánnos

Sun, wind and beautiful downward views

## Embaros – Miliarádon – Koúpa – Loutráki – Ano Viánnos

**Starting point:** Embaros.
**Walking times:** Embaros – Miliarádon 20 mins., Miliarádon – sheep farm 1½ hrs., sheep farm – mountain ridge ½ hr., mountain ridge – little church 50 mins., little church – Ano Viánnos 1 hr.; total time 4¼ hrs.
**Difference in height:** ascent 650m, descent 550m.
**Grade:** strenuous climb, a good sense of direction needed. Sun protection, provisions, water.
**Stops and accommodation:** tavernas and rooms in Ano Viánnos.
**Bus connections:** bus service to Ierápetra and Iráklion.

Embaros lies in the south-western foothills of the Díkti mountains. The region is closed off to the south by an imposing rock face below the 1187m high Koúpa.

Begin the walk in the main square of **Embaros**. Between the post office and the *kafeníon* a road leads to the east. After 100m a road sign indicates left to Miliarádon, but you carry straight on, past a little church, along the tiny street winding through the village. Four minutes later the road forks at a large electricity pylon. Go left here, then through the streambed and on the gravel road straight on up to **Miliarádon**. At the east side of the church, past a yellow post box, ascend the road of 28th October. This becomes a gravel-covered mule path after a *kafeníon*. Past some sheds after three minutes you step over a water pipe and just after that, a water channel. As you look back on the ascent there's a beautiful view of Embaros, Xeniákos and Miliarádon. Carry straight on at a junction, not right towards the rocks.

The path soon winds steeply up towards the rock face. Shortly afterwards at

*Ascent path above the sheer north face of Koúpa.*

a left-hand bend (a hollow with a tree stump) you will see a wall just above. Leave the broad path here on an ascending path which comes out at a gate. Having gone through the gate, continue the walk along the distinct path which crosses the gorge at the upper terraces. It climbs above the sheer rock face, goes above a cleft and continues up along the edge of the precipice until you come to a **sheep farm**. Past some feeding troughs on the left there's a short section uphill until the path forks. Take the left branch along beside a pipe towards the top of the mountain. From a water trough cross the slope to the left almost on the level until you reach the ridge coming down from the summit below a trig point. Descend the ridge in a south-easterly direction to some rocky spikes. The path swings to the left down towards three thin, wild pear trees and continues along the mountain ridge where the path forks about 200m before a large boulder. Continue right here. The path goes beside fence posts and keeping almost on the level, meets a gravel road which you follow downhill. Go through a double gate and beside a fence behind which a path branches off right as a shortcut. Take this to the **Agios Ioánnis chapel**.

Through an iron gate at the back of the chapel follow a path up the slope at first, then a path downhill that has a gorge on the left and a dry stonewall on the right. It crosses the gravel road and later on meets the road, which then changes over onto the other side of the gorge at a well. Past the little church of Agios Ioánnis, belonging to the village of Loutráki, walk along a tarmac road down to **Ano Viánnos**.

# 31 Ascent of Díkti, 2148m

From the Lassíthi plateau onto Díkti

## Avrakóndes – Díkti – Avrakóndes

**Starting point:** Avrakóndes-Koudoumaliá (south-eastern edge of Lassíthi plateau).
**Walking times:** Avrakóndes – chapel Panagia Limnakáro 1½ hrs., chapel – col a good 2 hrs., ascent of the south slope

1 hr., ascent of the south-west ridge 1 hr., summit – chapel a good 2½ hrs., chapel – Avrakóndes 1 hr.; total time 9 hrs.
**Difference in height:** ascent 1400m, descent 1400m.
**Grade:** difficult mountain walk demanding stamina, sure-footedness and best equipment. Possible only in stable weather (be aware of thunderstorms and old snow fields into May). E4 waymarkers in places.
**Stops and accommodation:** rooms and tavernas in villages in the Lassíthi plateau.
**Bus connections:** twice daily from Iráklion and Agios Nikólaos to the Lassíthi plateau (Psihró).
**Alternative:** the first 1½ hours can be shortened by taking a vehicle suitable for cross-country driving from Agios Geórgios: at the end of the village (road going in the direction of Agios Konstandínos) a 7km long gravel track branches off right and goes up to the plateau with the chapel of Panagia Limnakáro. It is just possible to drive along this road, but be careful after rain, when the ground is very soggy!

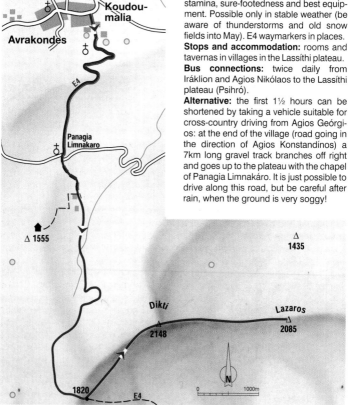

*View from the Lassíthi plateau of the Díkti mountains.*

Your starting point is the twin village of **Afrakóndes-Koudoumaliá**. A gravel road leads in a southerly direction round a wide bend out of the village and on the right past a sheep pen, continuing up the slope round steep bends. The old mule path (E4) goes uphill left after the first bend (green waymarkers). It crosses the first chain of hills after the plain, descends gently downhill onto a plain rising up to the Díkti massif and leads along the right-hand edge to the chapel of **Panagia Limnakáro**. Just after the chapel it is joined on the left by the roadway from Agios Geórgios and a little later from the right, by the roadway from Kimináki. The ascent leads straight on towards a farmstead. Directly by the farmhouse E4 posts indicate the ascent to the Stanestasi hut on the right above (1555m). Stay on the plain. In the background you can see the broad, rocky Díkti massif. The waymarked path goes towards the upper right-hand edge of the gravel plain, crosses a deep ditch, zigzags up the steep terrain and at an altitude of 1570m, reaches a flat **col**.

An old path, difficult to see, leads left over the steep west slope to the Dikti ridge. Stay on the E4, which goes at first rather precipitously to the south-east, then uphill again to the east. The E4 reaches the highest point at 1820m (at 200m intervals yellow E4 posts). From here ascend left following the yellow waymarkers to the west ridge. After about an hour's ascent you find yourself on the crest of the ridge that brings you up towards the Díkti summit. Go round the flatter south flank to avoid the steeper rocky sections. After an ascent of just under five hours you are standing on the highest peak of the Díkti massif, the 2148m high **Díkti**.

Hikers with enough stamina left can also take in the summit of Lázaros (2085m). The easy 'detour' leads directly along the ridge (1 hr.).

# 32 Onto Aféndis Hristós, 2141m

To the highest chapel in eastern Crete

## Col, 1570m – Aféndis Hristós – Avrakóndes

**Starting point:** Avrakóndes or col, 1570m (compare Walk 31).

**Walking times:** col – turn-off from E4 (1820m) 45 mins., turn-off from E4 – ridge 45 mins., ridge – summit 1 hr., descent depending on the condition of the snow 2½-4 hrs.; total time 5-6½ hrs. (Ascent and descent from Lassíthi plateau to the col another 3½ hrs.).

**Difference in height:** ascent 1600m, descent 1600m.

**Grade:** as in Walk 31, but longer and some difficult route finding over rough ground, lengthy stretches over slabs and loose rock. Be sure to wait for settled weather. The ascent is one of the most demanding walks on Crete. E4 waymarkers from the Lassíthi plateau to the start of the rough terrain.

**Stops and accommodation:** see Walk 31.

**Bus connections:** see Walk 31.

Just like the ascent of Díkti this ascent up Aféndis Hristós starts on the Lassíthi plateau. However, due to the length and difficulty of this mountain walk, it is recommended that you organize a drive up to the high plain (for the description of the ascent up to the col, see Walk 31).

Following the E4, after 2 ½ hours from the Lassíthi plateau, you reach the

*The steep north flank of Aféndis Hristós.*

highest point (1820m) of the E4. Before the hiking path turns off to the east (two waymarker posts are to be found at the same height at an interval of 200m), leave the path to the right and ascend, from now on over rough ground, in the direction of Aféndis Hristós.

After about 10 minutes you have an open view of the many peaks of the Aféndis massif. Over an earthy ridge, past the remains of an old shed, you come to the first steep slope and across this to a ridge (1990m). From this ridge there are faded 'red dots' halfway up on the left from the first summit. There are some cairns as well later on. Now either go through the hollows or, without losing height, westwards almost onto the summit until you can see the white summit chapel. You come to the summit of **Aféndis Hristós** over a steep rocky peak – only the chapel offers you shelter from the strong winds up at the top. A Minoan shrine is supposed to have stood here and they say that some old Minoan coins have been found there at church festivals.

The return is back the same way but, depending on the time of year, you can make the descent considerably easier by descending the widespread snowfields. However, be careful not to underestimate the frequent danger of collapsing snow in the late afternoon.

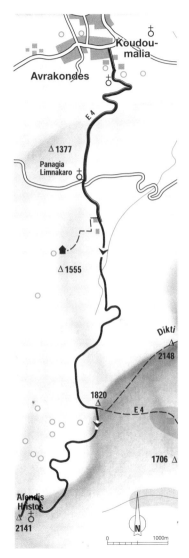

# 33 Through the Díkti mountains

From Selákano through the mountains to Lassíthi

### Hrístos – Selákano – Díkti mountains – Avrakóndes

**Starting point:** Hrístos, 500m, village to the east of the Díkti mountains, accessible from Ierápetra via Anatolí / Malés.

**Walking times:** Hrístos – Selákano 1¼ hrs., Selákano – end of the road 1¼ hrs., end of the road – rocky hill (oak wood) 45 mins., rocky hill – 2nd spring 45 mins., 2nd spring – col 40 mins. col – turn-off to Díkti 40 mins., turn-off – church 50 mins., church – Avrakóndes 1 hr.; total time 7-7½ hrs.

**Difference in height:** ascent 1400m, descent 1000m.

**Grade:** moderate mountain walk, in the upper regions narrow and, at times, bad paths where good route finding is needed. Partly in the shade, no water along the way in summer. E4 waymarkers throughout.

Safe weather conditions needed due to the length and altitude.

**Stops and accommodation:** a good choice of rooms and tavernas in Ierápetra and along the coast, especially in Mírtos. Basic overnight accommodation on the mountain pastures of Selákano: bunkhouse with 7 beds, key obtainable from the *kafeníon*.

**Bus connections:** once a day to and from Ierápetra.

A road, with a concrete surface at first, winds up the steep southern slope from the entrance to the village of **Hrístos** past the school building. High above a deep gorge it crosses into a narrow valley. The valley widens out and after a total of 1¼ hours you reach the extensive wooded area of **Selákano** at an altitude of about 1000m.

*Old snow in the Díkti mountains lingers into early summer.*

Formerly just a summer settlement – vegetables, fruit, nuts and a few vines were grown here – some new houses have now sprung up, next to the increasingly derelict houses, which allow occupation all year round.

About 100m before the first house carry straight on at the turn-off and a sign before the first building indicates to the left uphill (*E4 waymarker*). A concrete roadway leads through the scattered houses and orchards uphill, past

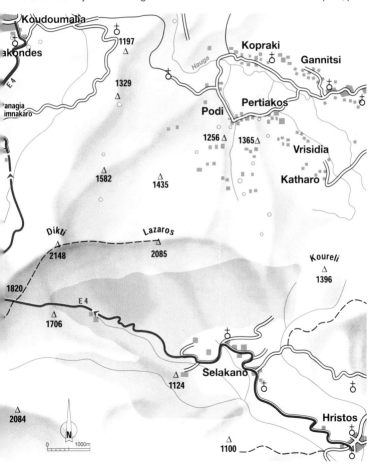

the communal building (telephone), across the concrete forecourt, towards a large fir tree standing in the middle of the roadway. 100m further on the footpath goes away from the road, straight across a field into a small valley. The path, which still has a paved surface in some places, heads left up towards some abandoned old buildings. Just before it ascends, follow a narrow path to the right (*yellow waymarkers*) which runs beside a dry streambed. The footpath arrives at a dirt road. Go a few metres to the right, climb about 1.5m higher onto the embankment and follow the path for about 150m to a terrace. Here go uphill left. After 50m you reach the old footpath again on the right (*E4 sign*). Go up a slope, through a gate and continue left along the gravel road. At the next junction the road going uphill ends at some sheds where you carry straight on.

The gravel path now runs over rocky ground through a thin fir and pine forest with many charred trunks. Leaving the cultivated land finally behind, you can already see the Aféndis Hristós massif towering up ahead.

The gravel road runs uphill round a gentle right-hand bend, but the narrow path (*yellow waymarkers*) leads left away from the road, up a gravel slope and crosses a road. Ascend the next road further uphill for about 15 minutes until it leads back eastwards after a narrow right-hand bend. From here it continues left along the bad road which ends at a field (1¼ hours to this point from the mountain pastures).

A well-marked path begins at the left edge of the field. It leads uphill, partly over the scree of the dry streambed, partly across the stony slope below

*Production of honey on the mountain pastures of Selákano.*

*The Díkti mountains (2148m).*

large oak trees and pines and then continues on the right edge of an increasingly narrow valley in a north-westerly direction with striking, polished rock formations above. Zigzag up a steep slope. At a height of 1500m you come to a **ridge** of rock with a large holm oak, an ideal place to stop for a breather. 10 minutes later you come past a stone basin with a small spring. A view opens up of the whole length of Aféndis Hristós. The path now ascends in the shade of large oak trees, mostly over rocky ground. Past some stone huts situated a little way from the path you reach a flat col. There's another slope to cross, then go past another contained spring to the next col. Here, at a height of 1700m, at the last tree, there's a small open place which allows you a wide view of the highest point of the path between Hristós and Díkti. Descend a little to the limestone hollows and shallow basins, then ascend again to the last and at the same time highest col (1820m) on your walk. From here there are distinct *E4 waymarkers* at an interval of 200m.

To the left goes over rough terrain to Aféndis Hrístos, but you follow the obvious path straight on down in the direction of **Lassíthi** (compare Walk 32). The yellow dots going uphill lead to the summit of Díkti (compare Walk 31).

# South-eastern Crete

*On the descent from the Asteroússia mountains to the south coast.*

The south coast of eastern Crete is one of the driest and sunniest regions on the island and Ierápetra claims to be the town with the most sunny days on Crete. Ierápetra, with its 10,000 inhabitants, is not only the largest town on the south coast, but is also one of the largest tourist centres, clearly evident from the huge hotel complexes and countless restaurants and cafés along the front and in the east of the town. In earlier times Ierápetra gained great importance as a trading town – Roman, Venetian and Turkish remains remind you of this fact today.

Along the narrow coastal strips on both sides of the town the early cultivation of fruit and vegetables has already been started in greenhouses and an artificial lake has been created at Gra Lignia for the watering of this 'plastic-covered' landscape. The beauties of nature are hardly visible any more in these areas.

On the thinly populated south coast between Léndas and Mírtos, at the foot of the Asteroússia mountains that drop steeply down to the sea, there's only an infrequent public transport service. So this is where many Crete fans, hoping to escape the hustle and bustle of mass tourism, have found their ideal spot. Along this section of coast you will discover Léndas with its informal tavernas, the forgotten Tsoútsouros or the village of Arvi, wedged in between banana plantations. Further inland in the Asteroússia mountains there are some beautiful walks to choose from, for example, onto Kófinas (1281m) or to the idyllic monastery of Koudoumá, situated by the sea. But there are also lovely walks along the Libyan Sea, for example, to the dragons' bay at Léndas, a sandy bay encircled by rocks, which has been taken over by sun-worshippers. Mírtos, 12km west of Ierápetra, is also a charming place to visit. Its appeal is not only the wide choice of rooms for rent, it also is an excellent starting point for walks in the mountains.

The countryside east of Ierápetra, along the road to Sitía, is over-developed. There are numerous small hotels and bed and breakfast places to choose from, but the beaches leave a lot to be desired. The main road beyond Makrigialos turns off inland, but before that, make a detour along the narrow coast road to Kápsa monastery. It's not possible to drive along the coastline beyond Goudourás.

The tiny island of Hrísi (Gaidourónisi) is a gem and accessible on a day trip by boat from Ierápetra. Cedars distorted by the wind, white sand dunes, crystal clear water and beaches strewn with tiny shells are the special features of this uninhabited island.

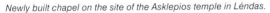

*Newly built chapel on the site of the Asklepios temple in Léndas.*

# 34 From Léndas to the dragons' bay

Thermal springs and the Asklepios shrine of Levin

**Léndas – Lutrá taverna – dragons' bay**

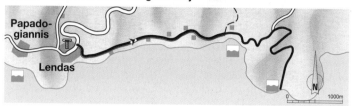

**Starting point:** Léndas, situated on the coast by some lovely beaches below the western Asteroússia mountain, reached from the Messará plain via Apessokári and Miamoú.

**Walking times:** Léndas – taverna 45 mins., taverna – col 20 mins., col – dragons' bay 30 mins., return 2 hrs.; total time 3¾ hrs.

**Difference in height:** 300m.

**Grade:** easy walk, no problems with route finding, only the steep descent into the gorge leads down along a narrow path. No shade, very hot in summer. Don't forget your swimming things.

**Stops and accommodation:** large choice of rooms for rent and tavernas in Léndas.

**Bus connections:** once a day in the tourist season to and from Iráklion and to and from Míres.

**Tip:** remains of the Asklepios temple above the village.

In the heyday of Górtys (4th century BC.) the inhabitants built an Asklépios temple in Léndas, the former Levin, next to the thermal springs which are still famous today for their healing powers. Léndas is a constantly growing, not especially attractive village on a grey shingle beach and makes a living from the many backpackers who come here by reason of its remoteness and the nearby beaches and bays.

From **Léndas** (on a right-hand bend with a signpost for 'Lutrá taverna') a gravel road runs across level ground, just above the coastline, and slowly ascends to the east. It continues through vegetable gardens and cultivated fields, with beautiful views down to the sea, in 45 minutes to the Lutrá taverna 3km away and situated 300m off the road (150m, accommodation, open from the end of April onwards).

Now descend a short way down to a beautiful bay enclosed by rocks. Along this ascend more steeply up a no longer used dirt road to a 150m high hill with a sweeping view along the coast eastwards and back to Léndas. A gravel road coming from the village of Krótos ends here. There's now a 10-minute descent on a narrow path, over a steep slope down into a narrow gorge.

*A rocky headland dropping down steeply into the sea separates the sandy beach from Léndas.*

This area is arid and rocky. Hardly any rain falls here all year round and the only vegetation to be found is grass, cistus, broom, thyme and sage. As a consequence the rock formations with their varying colours and hues are even more spectacular.

After about 15 minutes walking through the gorge the view opens out to the sea. You can see the deep blue water of the **dragons' bay** ahead, bordered on both sides by rocks. A pebbly beach with flat rocky slabs, over which the sea breaks, invites you to stop for a swim.

In high temperatures you are recommended to walk to the bay in the morning and not return until late afternoon.

# 35 From Krótos to Léndas

From the western Asteroússia mountains to beaches for a swim

### Krótos – Lutrá taverna – Léndas

**Starting point:** Krótos, 500m, small village on the southern slopes of the western Asteroússia mountains, 8km from Léndas.
**Walking times:** Krótos – Lutrá taverna 1½ hrs., Lutrá taverna – Léndas 1 hr.
Or: Krótos – dragons' bay 2½ hrs., dragons' bay – Lutrá taverna 1 hr., taverna – Léndas 45 mins.; total time 2½ hrs. or 4¼ hrs.
**Difference in height:** descent 500m or 650m, ascent 150m.
**Grade:** easy walk on the descent, good route finding, half along dirt or gravel roads. Very hot in summer.
**Stops and accommodation:** see Walk 34.
**Bus connections:** see Walk 34.
**Tip:** see Walk 34.

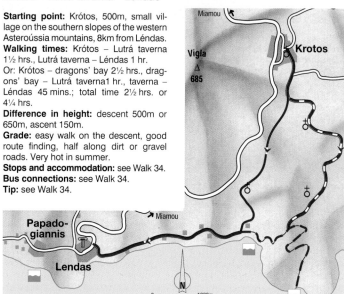

This relatively short and easy walk is recommended for those on a beach holiday in Léndas looking for something alternative and the chance to get to know the surrounding area.

**Krótos** lies at a height of 500m on the southern slopes of the mountain ridge and is reached by bus from Léndas. Descend from the road into the village below, continue down through the village and follow the roadway that leads out of the village southwards just below the tarmac road. Fenced-off orchards and olive trees accompany you at first. After about a kilometre the roadway leads onto a col and you descend right at the junction. The path now runs again through orchards, keeping to the right-hand side of the valley, and goes beside a telephone wire for a stretch of 2km. Keep right again at the next junction (*red waymarkers*).
The roadway continues descending at the right-hand edge of the valley and

*Coastal landscape below Lutrá taverna.*

crosses a steep rocky slope. On the other side of a narrow rocky gorge you can see a chapel built into the rocks. Then, after a bend, there's an open view down to the Lutrá taverna, still a distance away, beyond which there's a beautifully glistening bay. The path now goes above a chapel, towards a ridge. Descend the ridge towards the sea (southwards) and on the left below you can see the bay with the taverna. Stay on the ridge until you come to the telephone masts again in a hollow. Follow a narrow path on the left directly below the telephone line down to the nearby **taverna** (open from the end of April). It's worth walking down to the coast from here simply because of the marvellous location of the taverna. If you follow the road below the taverna eastwards you will come to a beautiful small bay in 5 minutes. The rest of the walk to Léndas goes along the gravel road to the west. It's 3.5km to the village.

**Alternative descent:** at the last junction above the steep rocky slope (immediately on the right a telephone mast with a *red dot*) you can follow the road left and come to the chapel mentioned above over the gorge. The road descends southwards along a ridge, east of and above the chapel, and reaches a small plateau at 150m above the sea. Leave the road there and follow the steep narrow footpath straight ahead down into a gorge (for the rest of the walk, see Walk 34).

# 36 Onto Kófinas, 1231m

Minoan summit shrine in the Asteroússia mountains

## Messará plain – Kapetaniená – Kófinas

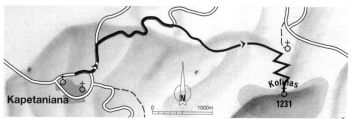

**Starting point:** Kapetaniená, situated 800m up above Loukía.

**Walking times:** Kapetaniená – plateau 1 hr., plateau – chapel 1 hr., chapel – summit 30 mins., descent 2 hrs.; total time 4½ hrs.

**Difference in height:** 430m.

**Grade:** easy, very rewarding mountain walk (exposed summit ascent over good rocky steps), good route finding. Possible all year round.

**Stops and accommodation:** in Míres and Féstos (Messará plain) restaurants, in Kapetaniená (upper village) rooms at Schuschnigg and bunk house with mattresses and cooking facilities or meals to order (tel.: 28930 41440).

**Bus connections:** once a day to Loukía.

From Loukía on the southern edge of the Messará plain an 8km long surfaced road zigzags up into the village of Kapetaniená. The village is in two parts and sits in a beautiful location on the steep southern slope of Kófinas.

Follow the gravel road which leads above the village, go left at the first turn-off and about 500m later carry straight on at another junction (the road leading uphill ends at some sheds). It winds up northwards onto a flat plateau which you reach after walking for an hour. Leave the road on a left-hand bend and follow an unclear path uphill. Past a dry streambed which is densely overgrown with oleander, continue uphill to the solitary **chapel** on the col north of Kófinas, 1100m. (You can also reach the col along the somewhat longer roadway which then continues south-eastwards down to the Koudoumá monastery).

Going past the chapel, follow the narrow, only intermittently marked path which is exposed and finally leads over some steep rocky steps (lack of vertigo essential) onto the narrow summit plateau and a bit further on to the **Kófinas** summit chapel.

The Minoans built a shrine up here, and a better panorama of south-eastern Crete and the Messará plain is unimaginable but there's an especially fabu-

*The ascent onto Kófinas goes along the left-hand edge of the picture over grass, gravel and rock.*

lous view of the monastery of Koudoumá situated way below and surrounded by blue sea.

# 37 To the monastery of Koudoumá

Cave churches and a remote monastery

## Kapetaniá – Agios Ioánnis – Agios António – Moni Koudoumá

**Starting point:** Kapetaniá, village in the Asteroússia mountains, situated at 800m, south of the Messará plain.

**Walking times:** Kapetaniá – rock barrier 1 hr., rock barrier – pebble beach 1¼ hrs., pebble beach – Agios António ¾ hr., Agios António – Koudoumá 50 mins.; total time 4 hrs., additional ½ hr. if you take the detour to the monastery at Agios Ioánnis.

**Difference in height:** descent 900m, ascent 100m.

**Grade:** moderate walk, some difficult paths over scree, so good footwear necessary. Very hot in summer, possible all year round, no drinking water along the way.

**Stops and accommodation:** Kapetaniá (see Walk 36) and Koudoumá monastery (easiest option).

**Bus connections:** see Walk 36.

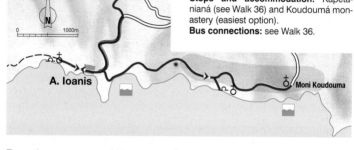

From the upper part of **Kapetaniá** descend the steep village street (accommodation in the last house on the left at Schuschnigg). Below the houses turn left towards the start of the road that leads to the cemetery. Continue along the road, turn off directly below the cemetery onto the old footpath that takes a considerable shortcut from the gravel road. Cross the road again at a gate (this leads round a hill on a wide right-hand loop) and continue your walk on the opposite side of the road through the gate. The old footpath descends on the left round the hill, thereby shortening more zigzag bends on the gravel road. At about a height of 550m, before a rock barrier, you again meet the road which you now stay on. It zigzags down the steep slope. You can see the group of houses of Agios Ioánnis a long way below. Half way below the belt of rock, at about a height of 280m, the old footpath branches off right downhill again. It leads down to the coast, with the last section along a gravel track again, and arrives at a several metre

*Both parts of Kapetanianá village in the Asteroússia mountains.*

high drop down to the sea. Go right along the road in 10 minutes to the village of **Agios Ioánnis**, and in another 10 minutes to the monastery of the same name. The village itself consists of a series of individual scattered houses which are only inhabited by fishermen in the summer.

Descend in the direction of Koudoumá a few metres left into the beautiful, long-drawn-out shingle bay. At its eastern edge there's a short ascent, then the footpath runs across an almost level terrace about 100m above the sea, through a very thin pine forest. At a junction about 30 minutes after the pebble beach (white marble cross with the inscription 'Agios Antónios') follow the narrow little path downhill on the right. The detour takes you past some bizarre rock formations and large pines down to the steep coast where the little church of **Agios Antónios** stands in an enormous cave. At the back of the cave you will find a limestone water basin and a pre-Christian place of worship. Back on the main path, walk partly under the trees, partly through low vegetation, in an easterly direction (there's a telephone line running parallel to the path). After half an hour you come to the edge of a canyon and 50m lower, below high trees and going towards the sea bordered by a beautiful shingle beach, you can see the large, well cared-for monastery of **Koudoumá** sprawling out in front of you. Monks still live here and just a little way from the monastery building there is some modest overnight accommodation available to tourists, with your own kitchen area (bring a sleeping bag with you). You can also reach the monastery along a zigzag road (only suitable for sturdy vehicles).

# 38 From Paránimfi to the monastery of Koudoumá

Walking along the old paths once used by the monks

### Paránimfi – Koudoumá

**Starting point:** Paránimfi, village situated at an altitude of 500m on the road coming from Harakás.
**Walking times:** Paránimfi – church 45 mins., church – descent into the gorge (junction) 1½ hrs., junction – gravel road 1½ hrs., gravel road – Koudoumá 1 hr.; total time 4¾ hrs.
**Difference in height:** descent 850m, ascent 250m.

**Grade:** moderate walk, for the most part on narrow, sometimes steep, paths with a lot of scree. Good route finding. Very hot in summer, no water along the way.
**Stops and accommodation:** tavernas and rooms in Harakás and Pírgos, modest accommodation (recommended that you take a sleeping bag) in Koudoumá monastery.
**Bus connections:** only as far as Harakás.

From Harakás at the south-eastern edge of the Messará plain a newly built tarmac road goes up onto the plateau in the Asteroússia mountains. Here at the top, in an extensive fertile hollow, is situated the village of **Paránimfi**. The road forks in the village – one branch goes in a south-easterly direction

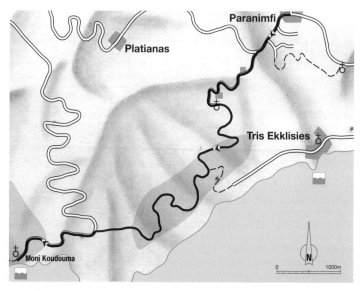

*Sunset at Koudoumá monastery.*

down to Tris Ekklisiés, the other in a westerly direction via the higher village of Platianás to Kapetaniná.

Follow the gravel road in the direction of Platianás, leading out from the upper edge of the village. After 1.5km, at a junction, a white marble cross indicates down to the left. Continue down the gravel road past some sheds and then up a steep slope until you come to a col. From here a narrow path (cairn) goes to the left leisurely downhill, passing close to the easily visible little **church** (well-preserved frescoes) to the start of the gorge and where the roadway also finishes. An old footpath leads into the gorge.

You now have a 600 vertical metre descent in front of you. At first the beautifully laid path zigzags down the left-hand side of the gorge, close to the rocks, with a fantastic view down to the sea. After 150 vertical metres the path changes across the bottom of the gorge onto the right-hand side and keeps on the level as it leads out of the gorge. There's a lovely view down to the village of Tris Ekklisiés from a small rock projection. After a few minutes you come to a junction and a white marble cross 'Koudoumá' indicates the direction again (the other path going down left leads to Tris Ekklisiés). The old partly paved path leads almost on the level, at a height of 320m, in a westerly direction and then ascends to a col, 500m. From here continue over a gentle up-and-down, crossing several smaller side valleys. You come to another rise of 500m, then descend through a treeless zone towards a gravel road coming from above. Along this, round several zigzag bends and a wide loop, you reach **Koudoumá monastery**. (To continue the walk, see Walk 37).

# 39 From Koudoumá to Tris Ekklisiés

Coastal path below the Asteroússia mountains

## Moni Koudoumá – Tris Ekklisiés

**Starting point:** Koudoumá monastery, situated below Kófinas beside the Libyan Sea and only reached along a very poor gravel track or by first following Walks 37 and 38.

**Walking times:** Koudoumá – start of the footpath 1½ hrs., footpath – turn-off to Tris Ekklisiés 1½ hrs., turn-off – gravel road 45 mins., gravel road – Tris Ekklisiés 45 mins.; total time 4½ hrs.

**Difference in height:** ascent 650m, descent 650m.

**Grade:** It is an easy walk with straightforward route finding, half of it on a gravel road and half on a footpath. Beautiful views down to the sea throughout.

Very hot in summer, little shade, no drinking water along the way.

**Stops and accommodation:** taverna in Tris Ekklisiés, modest overnight accommodation in Koudoumá (see Walk 38).

**Bus connections:** see Walk 38.

From **Koudoumá monastery** follow the gravel road which leads away from the sea round a wide bend. It goes eastwards across the southern slope of Kófinas, at first with a view of the huge 1200m high sheer face of Kófinas, then with constantly changing views down to the rocky coastline.

After 1½ hours you have reached a height of 450m and you leave the gravel road to the right and continue the walk along the old path. On a gentle up-and-down it crosses some small side valleys, twice reaches a height of 500m and runs time and again under the shade of large pine trees.

Eventually you reach a crossroads with a white marble cross. The subse-

*The well cared-for Koudoumá monastery.*

quent 45-minute descent leads round lots of bends to the narrow coastal strip with the dirt road you could already see from above. The almost level road running about 100m above the sea, brings you eastwards to **Tris Ekklisiés**. It takes about three quarters of an hour to the village which is wedged in at the foot of high rocks.

A twisting gravel road goes from Tris Ekklisiés up over the 500m high mountain chain to the village of Paránimfi and from there on to Harakás in the Messará plain.

# 40 On the plateau of Paránimfi

Views down to Tris Ekklisiés

### Paránimfi – precipice looking down to the south coast – Paránimfi

**Starting point:** Paránimfi, 600m, in the Asteroússia mountains (see Walk 38).

**Walking times:** Paránimfi – waterfall 40 mins., waterfall – edge of the precipice 15 mins., edge of the precipice – church 15 mins., church – Paránimfi 45 mins.; total time 2 hrs.

**Difference in height:** 200m.

**Grade:** easy round walk with beautiful views down to the sea, possible all year round.

**Stops and accommodation:** *kafeníon* in Paránimfi (see Walk 38).

**Bus connections:** see Walk 38, but it's best to use a car.

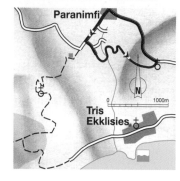

*On the south coast.*

*Views down into the dramatic, rugged mountain landscape of the south coast.*

This short round walk can be used as an exploratory walk before undertaking the strenuous descents to the south coast and gives you views of the wildly dramatic landscape of the Asteroússia mountains.

From **Paránimfi** you first follow the road in the direction of Platianás until about 300m later, a narrow dirt road turns off down to the left. The dirt road goes along the right-hand hillside, then through the valley bottom southwards, towards the visible rock barrier which marks the boundary of the high valley on the south side to the sea. At the next junction go right, through the fields, over a water channel towards the nearby rocks. The stream has cut a small ravine for itself; after rainfall a large waterfall plunges down to the coast over the rock face. A narrow footpath continues round a left-hand bend directly along the edge of the **edge of the precipice**. The view way down to the coast, 600m below, is stunning.

A little further on you can look down through a ravine to the small village of Tris Ekklisiés, which appears as if wedged between rocks and the blue line of the sea. Eventually you go eastwards over a flat-topped hill, on tracks or over rough ground, to the church visible above on the slope. It lies on the road linking Paránimfi with Tris Ekklisiés. Going right, past the church, the gravel road winds its way round countless zigzags down to Tris Ekklisiés, but you follow it to the left through the fields, on a wide loop to the north-west, back to **Paránimfi**.

# 41 To ancient Príansos

A mountain of churches

## Káto Kasteliyaná – Príansos – Káto Kasteliyaná

**Starting point:** Káto Kasteliyaná at the south-eastern edge of the Messará plain, on the road linking Pírgos – Skiniás.
**Walking times:** Káto Kasteliyaná – 1st chapel 50 mins., walk round the plateau 20 mins., descent 40 mins.; total time 2 hrs.
**Difference in height:** 250m.
**Grade:** easy walk, possible all year round. Advisable to wear long trousers owing to the dense vegetation on the hill.
**Bus connections:** twice a day from Pírgos.
**Stops and accommodation:** rooms and tavernas in Pírgos and Tsoútsouros.

A 420m high flat-topped circular hill rises at the south-eastern end of the 200m high Messará plain. There's a white chapel standing on the top which is visible from a long way off. Archaeologists found the remains of ancient Príansos on this well-located site. Its building style and its location point to a Dorian foundation, but later discoveries show that Príansos continued to be inhabited after that as well.

50m after the end of the village of **Káto Kasteliyaná** (in the direction of Pírgos) a path leads up to the cemetery. From the top you have a good view across the hill and of the easy to find ascent path which runs up almost in a direct line from the village to the remote chapel.

From the northern edge of the cemetery, on the side facing the hill, walk under olive trees for a short way without paths in the direction of Príansos and after about 100m go diagonally right down to the gravel road. Follow this left uphill and at the crossroads after 100m carry straight on up along the rutted path. Near a large high-tension pylon cross again over a gravel path (continuing straight on) and in places you can see the old paving stones of the path. At the next cross path go a few metres at first to the left, then right again and carry on downhill. The ascent path leads almost all the way through olive plantations and not until you are further up the hill does it become more overgrown (long trousers are an advantage here). Now go a few metres to the left through a gate. About 60m after that you come to a small, flat terrace with an old church.

*One of the churches of ancient Príansos.*

Through another small gate you now keep right as you ascend the hill and go round the almost circular, flat summit plateau. You come across decaying walls, ruins, several cisterns and another very old chapel on the walk round **Príansos** – all of this evidence of a large former settlement. Then, at the highest point, there are also some remains of a big church from where you have the most beautiful panorama of the Messará plain.

The descent goes down past the white chapel located on the east side, in a southerly direction. 150m after the chapel you leave the fenced hill through a gate in the wire netting and following the gravel road, walk back along the path you came on to the village.

# 42 From Kastelianá to Tsoútsouros

Hiking and swimming near ancient sites

## Káto Kastelianá – Tsoútsouros

**Starting point:** Káto Kastelianá, 200m, in the south-east of the Messará plain.

**Walking times:** Káto Kastelianá – chapel 45 mins., chapel – descent of the valley 45 mins., valley – Tsoútsouros 1½ hrs.; total time 3-3½ hrs.

**Difference in height:** ascent 250m, descent 450m.

**Grade:** easy valley walk mostly in the dry streambed, good footwear necessary. No drinking water, very hot in summer.

**Stops and accommodation:** numerous rooms and tavernas in Tsoútsouros.

**Bus connections:** only as far as Káto Kastelianá (see Walk 41).

**Tips:** cave of the Eileithyia cult (goddess of birth), articles which have been found there are on display in the archaeological museum in Iráklion, excavation of an Archaeo-Mycenaean settlement.

From **Káto Kastelianá** an 11km long tarmac road goes over the foothills of the Asteroússia mountains and leads down to a beautiful shingle beach and the steadily growing village of Tsoútsouros. Walk the first three kilometres along the road uphill to a small **chapel** which is situated just before the top of the ridge (450m). Leave the road here and follow a dirt road across the western slope. Below you can see a long-drawn-out valley running southwards, densely overgrown with oleander.

Half way down the slope there's a shepherds' hut and a bit lower down some more ruins. Following a narrow path you descend past both the houses diagonally left, always heading towards the valley bottom. At a large solitary olive tree you come to the dry gravel streambed of the valley. Keep going down the valley at first in the dry streambed, then on the right or left of the trickling stream. The valley is at first very flat and wide. The nearer you come to the sea, the closer the slopes of the valley come together. Rock formations come into view and the last section goes through a small gorge. When the water level is high you will find some pools in which you can take a

*The green emerald lizard is one of the most beautiful reptiles on the island.*

swim and with a bit of luck you'll also see some freshwater crabs. The gorge suddenly opens out and going past sheep pens and some ruins you reach the first houses of **Tsoútsouros**. Countless tavernas, some of which are still being built, rooms for rent, bars and discos form a strange contrast to this remote region.

The **cave of worship** is to be found at the point where the road meets the sea, after the row of houses in the rocks. The excavation site nearby to the west is a 10-minute walk.

*Seen from afar – Agios Stávros chapel.*

# 43 From Tsoútsouros to Agios Nikitás

Coastal walk to the Byzantine church in the rock

## Tsoútsouros – Maridáki – Agios Nikitás

**Starting point**: Tsoútsouros, coastal village east of the Asteroússia mountains, linked to the Messará plain via an 11km long tarmac road.

**Walking times**: Tsoútsouros – Maridáki 1 hr., Maridáki – Agios Nikitás 45 mins., Agios Nikitás – bay 10 mins., return via chapel 2 hrs.; total time 4 hrs.

**Difference in height**: 250m.

**Grade**: easy coastal walk on good paths,

except for an exposed section.
Very hot in summer, ideally combined with a swim.

**Stops and accommodation:** rooms and tavernas in Tsoútsouros, taverna in Maridáki, modest overnight accommodation and drinking water in the monastery of Agios Nikitás.

**Bus connections:** see Walk 42.

**Tip:** see Walk 42.

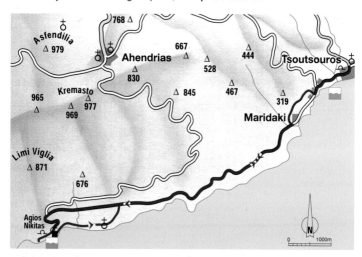

**Tsoútsouros**, visited by tourists in the first place because of its beautiful pebble beach and its tranquillity and remoteness, offers lovers of nature interesting and diverse surroundings. One of the most impressive walks goes below the rugged mountains, keeping close to the sea, to the monastery of Agios Nikitás.

Follow the gravel road out of the village which goes west along the beach into the neighbouring bay. After the houses there you will see the excavation site of Inatós. The last house, a taverna, has been built close to the

*View from the monastery garden to Agios Stávros chapel.*

rocks and the hiking path begins directly after it. The old path leads steeply up onto a terrace of land, about 70m above the sea, then there's an almost level section, accompanied by the water pipe and a telephone line. The terrain becomes narrower, rocks get closer together and the view opens out ahead into a narrow rocky bay, to the houses of **Maridáki**. Climb up 140m and then the narrow and airy path leads down over rocks into the small village.

Continue westwards along the gravel road on the other side. Barren slopes are now predominant. After about 3km you will see on the left a small peninsula with a trig point and ahead, on the next col, the brilliant white chapel of **Agios Stávros**. The road leads past it and above and forks after another kilometre at a stream crossing. Follow the bad path downhill towards the coast. The site of **Agios Nikitás** monastery looms up unexpectedly ahead after a bend – a green oasis with terraced fields, trees, flowers, white-washed houses and a Byzantine church at the foot of the black rocks. Going down through the garden you come to a small gate and after a 10-minute steep descent into a wonderful, narrow pebbly bay – an inviting place for a swim.

The return path goes along a narrow path at first that leads, 20m from the monastery grounds, across the gravel bed of the stream. An old footpath continues on the other side. It leads down through rocks, going round the steep precipices to the sea, then up the slope to the solitary chapel of **Agios Stávros**. From there you can enjoy an almost infinite view along the coast. Now climb up to the roadway and return to **Tsoútsouros** back the way you came.

# 44 The Sarakinas gorge at Mírtos

Where Mírtos stream squeezes through narrow rocks

## Mírtos – Míthi – Sarakinas gorge – Míthi

**Starting point:** Míthi at Mírtos.
**Walking time:** 1½ hrs.
**Difference in height:** 50m.
**Grade:** the hiking path leads partly through the water (additional gym or bathing shoes are recommended). Some scrambling over smooth boulders (for experienced mountaineers).
**Bus connections:** six times daily Ierápetra – Mírtos or Míthi.
**Stops and accommodation:** tavernas and rooms in Mírtos, *kafeníon* in Míthi.

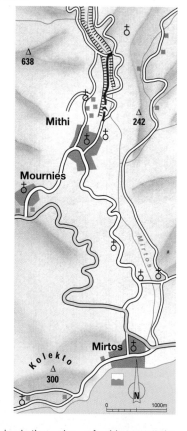

In summer when the sun shines without mercy down onto the south coast of Crete and everyone is dying of thirst, holidaymakers in Mírtos should take a trip to the small village of Míthi where the nearby Mírtos stream forces its way through high, polished rocks before finding its way in a broad gravel bed into the Libyan Sea.

You come to **Míthi** if you follow the main road from Ierápetra in the direction of Mírtos and continue to Míthi. From there drive another 1km towards Máles, until you reach the Mírtos streambed.

50m before the streambed a path goes off left to a **dam wall** where your walk begins. Ten metres further along there's a former mill channel along which you come to the start of the gorge. You will need to remove your shoes at the first opening in the rocks – refreshing to say the least – especially in the spring when the snow melts in the Díkti mountains and the water is still icy cold, but you also have to be prepared for a strong current. Under certain circumstances the gorge is even impassable. There are some smooth boulders to climb over which might give the hiker a few problems, but that only helps to increase the delightful adventure of this walk.

You can get round a waterfall on the left through a cave and climbing over a smooth tree trunk to then slip out through a narrow rock window. Just before the end of the narrow section there's a waterfall, about 3m high, which has to be climbed from a pool using bridging technique (II), and right at the end a rigid metal ladder. After about an hour you come to the end of the gorge. If you climb up right, you meet a gravel path which brings you back to the road to Máles. Return along this to your starting point. You can also walk through the stony Mírtos riverbed back into the village of the same name (4km).

*Sarakinas gorge – an adventurous path through narrow gorges.*

# 45 From Mourniés to Máles

Below the eastern Díkti mountains

### Mourniés – Míthi – Metaxohóri – Hrístos – Máles

**Starting point:** Mourniés at Mírtos.
**Walking times:** Mourniés – Míthi ½ hr.,
Míthi – Metaxohóri 2 hrs., Metaxohóri –
Hrístos ¾ hr., Hrístos – Máles 1 hr.; total
time 4¼ hrs.
**Difference in height:** 450m.
**Grade:** strenuous, but easy mountain
walk with lovely views.
Sun protection, provisions and drinking
water.
**Bus connections:** six daily Ierápetra –
Mírtos; Máles – Ierápetra at 14.30.
**Stops and accommodation:** tavernas
and rooms in Mírtos. Tavernas in Míthi and
between Hrístos and Máles. *Kafeníon* in
Mourniés and Máles.
**Alternative routes:** you can also start this
walk in Míthi.
The link Walk 33 goes from Hrístos onto
Dikti.

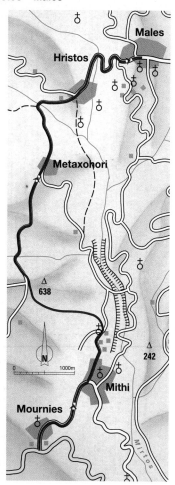

A curious thing is to be found in the
main square in **Mourniés –** the anti-
quated coffee bar 'Mournia', a small
blue-painted shop. The inside is
dark and smelling of mothballs. If
you're not in a rush to have a cup of
coffee, you will find one later in
Míthi.
You can reach Mourniés by bus or
taxi from Mírtos. From the main
square follow the road to the right,
which after a few minutes takes you
out of the village. You are surrounded by almond and olive trees.
Ignore a road joining from the left.
After a 30-minute descent you arrive in **Míthi**.
Follow the road into the village and
there are several signposts where it

126

*At the start of the walk in Mourniés.*

starts to go downhill again. About 10m before this forest of signs there's a turning off left onto a road going steeply uphill which branches off right after a few metres. At the last houses, at the end of a concrete section of path, carry straight on past a flat concrete roof. Soon afterwards the path forks again where you continue up to the left. From now on you have a beautiful view of the valley lying below with the broad riverbed that flows into the sea at Mírtos. Fifteen minutes after the end of the village of Míthi the path goes high above the deep-cut Sarakinas gorge and makes a 180-degree turn so that you can see Míthi again in front of you. The path ends five minutes later and an ascending path continues beside the fence. Cairns mark the way into a fenced stand of pine trees which you enter through a gate. Over slightly rocky ground you come to a lovely viewpoint from where you can look down onto the steep walls of the Sarakinas gorge below, and in the distance you can see the houses of Máles on the mountain hillside. A good one hour after Míthi you go through a side valley with a magnificent view into the gorge. On the opposite side the path winds uphill round steep bends. The ascent takes 25 minutes, then the ground levels out again.

Go through a gate and with very few paths, head towards the hill situated in front of you. Cairns help you with route finding. You arrive at a threshing circle past which there's a roadway. Swing right onto this (soon a

*Gorge on the way from Míthi to Metaxohóri.*

*Countryside between Hrístos and Máles.*

white-washed house appears further down) and you walk in a north-westerly direction, almost on the level, to **Metaxohóri**, which you reach in half an hour. Many of the houses are abandoned and have fallen into decay. Go right through the village and down the road that leads over to the village of **Hrístos** which you can already see lying ahead. Only some time after an old church do you come to the sign for the village. Take the left-hand higher path which leads you up round a left bend to the entrance to the village where a tarmac road also begins. A few hundred metres later the roadway turns off left to Selákano mountain pastures (see Walk 33), but you carry straight on. The panoramic road allows you a beautiful view of the far-distant sea. Before a big left-hand bend you come past the Agia Paraskevi taverna. It stands under shady plane trees (spring water) and has a large terrace. Since Máles only has a modest choice of restaurants, you should avail yourself of the opportunity of buying something to eat or drink here, that's if you've got enough time before catching the bus.

Before the entrance to **Máles** a sign points the way to Míthi, and this is the dusty road you take if you have to go back there, but the bus ride is more pleasant, even if there is a change of buses. The bus from Ierapetra arrives in Máles at 14.30 and turns back immediately.

# 46 To the summit chapel of Estavroménos, 951m

From Ierápetra into the mountain forests of the eastern Díkti mountains

## Anatolí – Estavroménos

**Starting point:** Anatolí, mountain village, 650m, on the road linking Malés – Kalamáfka.
**Walking times:** Anatolí – col 1 hr., col – summit chapel 20 mins., return 1 hr.; total time 2½ hrs.
**Difference in height:** 350m.
**Grade:** easy mountain walk, sporadic waymarkers, good route finding. Partly in the shade, possible all year round.
**Stops and accommodation:** large choice of rooms and tavernas in Ierápetra and the villages along the coast, *kafeníon* in Anatolí.
**Bus connections:** daily to Anatolí and return possible.
**Tip:** collection of icons in the church of Anatolí; the village of Kalamáfka is also worth seeing.

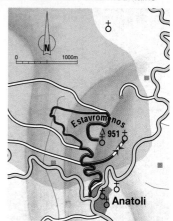

Coming from Ierápetra, a 12km long road goes from Gra Lignia up into the mountain village of **Anatolí**. The drive through the bizarre mountain landscape is an experience in itself.

The road forks at the entrance to the village, opposite a small shelter (in front of it there's a tap with excellent drinking water). This is where the walk begins. Follow the concrete road steeply uphill and at the first junction turn towards the gravel road ascending left (at the next long bend you can take a shortcut via a footpath branching off left). The gravel road goes round several bends towards the rocky peak of Estavroménos and for a short time the white summit chapel can also be seen – a marvellous mountain landscape with picturesque rock formations and enormous old pine trees. Cross over a broader gravel road (the chapel Agia Paraskeví is 300m away on the right) and follow the old gravel path uphill (*cairn*). At the next junction, too, stay on the old ascending gravel path. It heads towards the nearby rocks of Estavroménos (*cairn*; although in a very wide loop, the road on the left also goes from the north onto the col before the summit section structure). The now narrow footpath, still paved in places, goes beneath tall trees, near to the steep rocks, westwards round the rocky summit and along a small

*The hidden chapel of Agia Paraskeví.*

stream to two tall charred tree stumps. Here you turn off from the more obvious path and climb up to the right (several cairns and sporadic red dots indicate the way).

Across a large clearing and past an old threshing circle as well as an old cistern, you reach a flat col at a height of 850m. You meet the gravel road again here. It leads in a loop, past spectacularly rugged rocks and bizarre fir trees and pines shaped by the wind, to the highest point of **Estavroménos** with the summit chapel, 951m. The view reaches across the extensive wooded landscape in the west up to the high peaks of the Díkti mountains. In the east you can see the plain of Ierápetra with the reservoir and the glistening sea of greenhouses.

The **return** is back the same way. On the way back you should plan a short detour to the Agia Paraskeví chapel, which lies hidden, and a visit to Anatolí church (a little way below the main road). This large and very beautiful church has an extensive collection of old icons from the surrounding, sometimes dilapidated churches and monasteries. You can fetch the key from the priest who lives in the first house on the right after the fork. A drive back via the large village of Kalamáfka, set in a particularly lovely location, is also be recommended.

# 47 In the area around Plakokéfala

From the Minoan site of Olerós to the church of Agia Panajía Vyromeni

## Messeléri – Agia Panajía

**Starting point:** Messeléri (400m), large village to the west of Plakokéfala on the road linking Ierápetra – Makriliá – Kaló Horió.

**Walking times:** Messeléri – end of the valley 40 mins., end of the valley – Agia Panajía 45 mins., Panajía – mountain col 30 mins., mountain col – Stavrós a good 1¼ hrs.; total time 3½ hrs.

**Difference in height:** 300m.

**Grade:** easy walk on gravel roads, E4 waymarkers, plenty of shade. Possible all year round.

**Stops and accommodation:** rooms and tavernas in Ierápetra and on the coast, *kafeníon* and taverna in Messeléri.

**Bus connections:** three times a week with a return journey possible too.

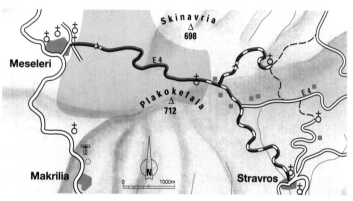

A newly extended road leads out of Ierápetra in a northerly direction through the village of Makriliá to Messeléri, 12km away in the mountains on the eastern edge of the Díkti massif. The large village lies in a very wide valley bottom. An abundance of water and a dense covering of trees characterize this fertile region which was inhabited as far back as the Minoan age. Olerós, one of the large Minoan towns, is presumed to have been located here. Although the area has not been systematically excavated, some discoveries point to that fact.

If you come from Ierápetra, a narrow road after a small bridge and before the first houses of **Messeléri**, leads into a dry streambed on the right (first *E4-waymarker*). Walk a fair distance along the edge of the village lying on the left, past the houses built close to one another and surrounded by small, lush gardens. A dense pinewood defines the scene on the right that

*Messeléri in front of the wooded chain of hills of Plakokéfala.*

stretches up as far as the rocks of Plakokéfala. Then you see the cemetery ahead with the chapel. At the road junction keep right, directly beside the cemetery. The road goes in an easterly direction through intensively cultivated orchards and plantations and slowly ascends to the head of the valley. It eventually winds up round several zigzag bends out of the valley bottom through dense pine forest and gets closer to the crags. A small basin-shaped valley opens up unexpectedly with many bizarre tall pines and rock formations. It is enclosed by the rock faces of Plakokéfala and Skinávria. In the middle, on a large rock, stands the church of **Agia Panajía Vyromeni** (610m). The old part of the church dates from the 14th century and possesses some very well preserved frescoes. The whole of the church site is presently being renovated (it's possible to look round the church on request, key in Messeléri).

The **return** is back the way you came. If you want to walk on further to Stavrós, follow the gravel road uphill, past old houses, sheds and a threshing circle. At a height of 700m, almost the height of the summit, you reach a col. At the junction here with the *E4 waymarkers* go right (following the *red waymarker* to the left would go to the chapel of Plakokéfala, compare Walk 48). The descent to Stavrós takes about 1½ hours (the E4 waymarkers lead to Vasiliki).

# 48 To the summit chapel of Agios Stavroménos

Above Ierápetra and the gulf of Mirabello

## Stavrós – Agios Stavroménos

**Starting point:** Stavrós (200m), 4km north of Ierápetra, at the foot of Plakokéfala.
**Walking times:** Stavrós – Agios Antónius 30 mins., Agios Antónius – gravel road 30 mins., gravel road – steep ascent 1 hr., descent via road – Stavrós 2 hrs.; total time 4 – 4½ hrs.
**Ascent:** 600m, descent 600m.

**Grade:** moderate mountain walk, partly over pathless terrain. Good footwear and long trousers necessary. No drinking water along the way, very hot in summer.
**Stops and accommodation:** see Walk 47, taverna and *kafenión* in Stavrós.
**Bus connections:** twice a week with return journey possible.

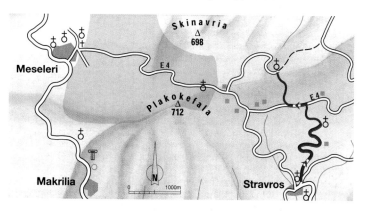

At the narrowest part of Crete, between the gulf of Mirabello and Ierápetra, lies a chain of hills, whose highest point is Plakokéfala (712m). The small chapel of Agios Stavroménos stands on the summit ridge to the east of it with a viewpoint par excellence.
**Stavrós,** a village worth a visit, situated close to the steep hills with its tiny crooked and narrow streets, is the starting point for your walk. In the upper part of the village you will find a small square with a well and a *kafenión*. From here follow the steep lane uphill which leads to a church and continues on the right out of the village. About 100m after the last houses just before the greenhouses, an old path, which is poor in places, winds up left. After about 15 minutes you cross over a gravel road which you meet again later on.

*Stavrós, from where you start the walk to the summit chapel.*

Now continue along the gravel road until it ends in front of the chapel of **Agios Antónius**. The chapel was built below an overhanging rock and on the left after the rock there's a spring. A narrow path continues on the right from the overhanging rock (cairn) and leads across several terraces with olive trees towards a building with a concrete cistern. Go past it and just above and reach a ruin situated further up and the gravel road 50m away. Follow this to the left (westwards, *E4 waymarker*). Already after about 200m, after a fenced-off plantation, leave the road and climb up to a newly built house. You will find yourself on rough terrain from now on. Climb up over old terraces behind the house to a scree slope. On the right of **Agios Stavroménos** chapel (it is clearly visible above the rocks) a fairly level cleft allow you to pass through into a hollow only a few metres below the chapel. It's now quite an exhausting climb up over boulders to the chapel. If you don't fancy this more adventurous route, you can always continue along the gravel road. It leads in a wide loop onto a col at the height of the summit (*E4 waymarkers*, see Walk 47).

At a turn-off marked with *red arrows* follow the gravel road to the right onto the north side of the ridge. From there it descends a short way and ends on the north side of and below the chapel. A footpath leads further up to the little church.

The panorama is magnificent. In the north you can see Agios Nikólaos and the gulf of Mirabello, in the west the Díkti mountains, in the south lies Ierápetra, almost near enough to reach out and touch, and in the east the mountains of Thriptís and Oros.

The **descent** is back the way you came. However, you could also descend to the west (compare Walk 47) or to the north (without paths down to the gravel road visible from above to Faneroménis, compare Walk 7).

# 49 Péfki gorge near Makrigialós

Ascent to Agios Stéfanos and back through Péfki gorge

## Makrigialós – Agios Stéfanos – Péfki – Makrigialós

**Starting point:** Makrigialós.
**Walking times:** Makrigialós – Agios Stéfanos 1½ hrs., Makrigialós – Péfki 1 hr., Péfki – Makrigialós 2¾ hrs., total time 5¼ hrs.
**Difference in height:** 450m.
**Grade:** sturdy footwear necessary, very

hot in summer, sun protection, drinks, provisions.
**Stops and accommodation:** hotels and rooms along the coast from Ierápetra to Makrigialós.
**Bus connections:** bus from Ierápetra to Makrigialós (30 mins.).

The route through the Péfki gorge goes along an old link path which used to connect the inhabitants of the mountain village with the coast roads, but is hardly used today.

Start the walk on the main road in **Makrigialós** at the signpost to Agios Stéfanos and go inland at first along this road. After just under 20 minutes, at a little church, a path branches off left. Fifteen minutes later take a turning off right uphill. You meet a cross path which you follow to the left. At the next fork go right. As you ascend you will see the remains of an old mule path, the main part of which has been covered by the present road. You soon come to the tarmac road. Take a shortcut from a bend in the road by going steeply uphill diagonally opposite. When you reach the tarmac road again, continue the path uphill on the other side to take another shortcut across the bends in the road. After about 30m going left along the road, turn right on a bend onto an old path enclosed by walls. There's a last view back of Makrigialos down on the coast. As you continue the walk you can see Péfki church on a rock in the middle of the valley ahead.

After 1½ hours you reach the houses of **Agios Stéfanos**. At the church in the middle of the village a signpost indicates the way to **Péfki**, where you will arrive after another hour's walk along the road. About 100m before the village there's a map with the gorge marked on it. This is the exact point where you start the return through the gorge after a rest in the village.

The paved path joins a track after about 500m to then continue left again between olive trees. Cross over a streambed. The terrain now opens out along the well-marked path between pine trees and after about half an hour you reach a picnic spot equipped with a set of wooden seats. Further along you come to the site of an old mill. A bit later at a junction, arrows point the way into the gorge.

After about 50 minutes some signposts indicate a waterfall. Left goes down into the gorge and a path leads right to the waterfall. After taking a quick look at the waterfall continue steeply downhill along the gorge path. Cross the side-stream and then the path goes down into the main streambed. You need to use a little skill to find your way round and over some of the obstacles, but it gets easier with the appearance of a handrail on the right. The construction of iron ladders helps you climb down two of the more difficult sections.

Cross over the streambed again before leaving the gorge. Another information board has been put up here. Continuing right brings you across the streambed over the stones to the other side. You have been walking for two hours in the gorge before you can see the extensive coastal plain ahead. Carry straight on, ignore a turn-off to the left and at a cross path head left towards the sea. Shortly afterwards you reach the tarmac road to Agios Stéfanos and return along this back to **Makrigialós**.

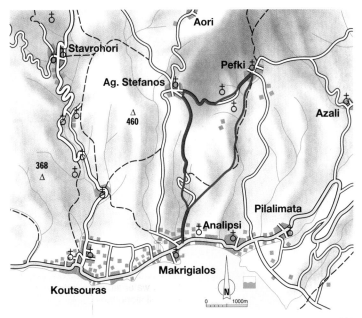

# 50 Walking and swimming on the island of Hrísi (Gaidourónisi)

A paradise for beach walkers and shell collectors

### Landing stage – Gold Beach – lighthouse – landing stage

**Starting point:** landing stage on the harbour promenade in Ierápetra.
**Walking times:** landing stage – Gold Beach 5 mins.; (walk round the eastern tip 1 hr.); Gold Beach – light house 1¼ hrs.; return 1 hr.; total time 2¼ hrs.
**Difference in height:** 20m.
**Grade:** easy walk. Sun protection, and depending on conditions, provisions and

drinking water.
**Boat connections:** The boat leaves Ierápetra at 10.30. Return from Hrísi at 16.30.
Several boats in the tourist season. No service in rough seas.
**Stops and accommodation:** restaurants and rooms in Ierápetra. Two tavernas on Hrísi.

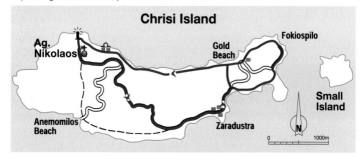

Chrisi Island

There are barely two dozen people waiting at the landing stage on the harbour promenade in **Ierápetra** at the end of April to catch a boat to the small island of **Hrísi** or Gaídouronisi (donkey island), as it's also called. The crossing takes about an hour. As you have to be back at the boat for 16.30, time is limited. But it's enough to get a good impression of the island with its marvellous shell beaches and cedar trees. A walk round the eastern tip is recommended and also the exploration of the north beach as far as the light house. There's a path from there through the interior of the island back to the landing stage.

You will have more time if you go straight from the landing stage over to **Gold Beach**. A path marked at the start with two rows of whitewashed stone leading through dunes of fine sand and knotty, wind-twisted cedars, brings you there in 5 minutes. At the beach turn to the left and go over rock partly eroded by the sea with little salt pans and fossilized shells, sometimes through soft sand. Loads of millimetre-sized shells form bright lines in the

*Path to Gold Beach. In the background the south coast near Ierápetra.*

sand. But you can find other shells as well, the shell cases from sea urchins and small starfish. The whole of the island is so flat that it can almost be washed over by the sea.

After an hour you arrive at a house. After that you see the small **beacon** which you will reach, going past the chapel of **Agios Nikólaos**, after another 20 minutes. A path goes from the lighthouse through the centre of the island back to the landing stage. The southern coastline is rockier than in the north and more difficult underfoot. Shell collectors will not have any luck there.

# Index

## Geographical

| | |
|---|---|
| jeojrafikós chartis | map |
| póli | town |
| chorió | village |
| spíti, spítia | house, houses |
| eklissía, eklissáki | church, chapel |
| dhromos | street, road |
| monopáti | path |
| strofí | bend |
| stavrodhrómi | wayside cross |
| wunó | mountain |
| katariji | mountain hut |
| korifí | peak, summit |
| hióni | snow |
| petres | stones, rocks |
| farángi | gorge |
| spiljá | cave |
| pedhiáda | plain |
| potamós | river |
| límni | lake |
| thálassa | sea |
| pijí | spring |
| dhéndhro, dhásos | tree, forest |
| lulúdhi | flower |
| prówata | sheep |
| katzíkes | goats |
| skílos | dog |
| pulí | bird |

## Food, accommodation and transport

| | |
|---|---|
| xenodhochío | hotel |
| krewáti | bed |
| lutró, dus | shower |
| faí | food |
| psomí | bread |
| kréas | meat |
| psári | fish |
| tirí | cheese |
| féta | sheeps' cheese |
| frúta | fruit |
| eliés | olives |
| ládhi | oil |
| aláti | salt |
| pipéri | pepper |
| neró | water |
| krasí | wine |
| chimós | juice |
| kafés | coffee |
| tsai | tea |
| hiliómetro | kilometre |
| avtokínito | car |
| leoforío | bus |
| isitírio | ticket |
| stási | stop |

## General phrases

| | |
|---|---|
| woíthia | help |
| parakaló, oríste | please |
| evcharistó | thank you |
| signómi | excuse me |
| kaliméra | hello |
| kaliníchta | good night |
| adhío | goodbye |
| símera | today |
| ávrio | tomorrow |
| chtes | yesterday |
| póte? | when? |
| pu? | where? |
| póso? | how much? |
| ti? | what? |
| makriá | far |
| kontá | near |
| psilá | high |
| hamilá | low |
| káto | below |
| páno | above |
| krio | cold |
| sestó | warm |
| fotinó | light |
| skótino | dark |
| ftinó | cheap |
| akriwó | expensive |

| Aα | Aa | Bβ | Bb | Χχ | Gg | Δδ | Th | Εε | Ee | Zζ | Zz |
|----|----|----|----|----|----|----|----|----|----|----|----|
| Hη | Jj | Θθ | Th | Iι | Jj | Kk | Kk | Λλ | Ll | Μμ | Mm |
| Nν | Nn | Ξξ | Xx | Oo | Oo | Ππ | Pp | Pρ | Rr | Σσ | Ss |
| Tτ | Tt | Yυ | Ii | Φφ | Ff | Χχ | Ch | Ψψ | Ps | Ωw | Oo |